THIS AWESOME BEN 10 BOOK BELONGS TO

....

AND I SWEAR TO HELP BEN TENNYSON KICK SOME ALIEN BUTT!

EGMONT
We bring stories to life

First published in Great Britain 2011 by Egmont UK Limited
239 Kensington High Street, London W8 6SA

ISBN 978 1 4052 5823 4
47413/1
Printed in Italy

EVER WISHED LIFE COULD BE MORE INTERESTING? THEN BE CAREFUL WHAT YOU WISH FOR ...

BEN 10

AGE 10

BEN TENNYSON IS ABOUT TO DISCOVER A WHOLE WORLD OF POWERS BEYOND HIS WILDEST DREAMS! PACKED WITH AWESOME ADVENTURES, A SECRET UNIVERSE AWAITS ...

SO, WHAT ARE YOU WAITING FOR? LET'S GET GOING!

WHERE DOES IT BEGIN?

BEN TENNYSON

Accidental Hero

THE STORY BEGINS WITH 10-YEAR-OLD BEN TENNYSON. BEN WAS LOOKING FORWARD TO A SUMMER ON THE ROAD WITH HIS GRANDPA MAX – UNTIL HIS COUSIN GWEN SHOWED UP! STILL, A SPECIAL DISCOVERY WILL MAKE IT A SUMMER LIKE NO OTHER ...

PERSONALITY

BEN'S A TYPICAL 10-YEAR-OLD BOY. HE'S INTO PLAYING SUMO SLAMMERS, AND GOOFING ABOUT. HOWEVER HARD HE TRIES (NOT VERY HARD!), BEN CAN'T STAY OUT OF MISCHIEF.

STRENGTHS

BEN'S FIERCELY LOYAL, AND WILL DO WHATEVER HE CAN TO PROTECT HIS FAMILY FROM HARM. HE'S ALSO PRETTY FEARLESS – EVEN WHEN HE DOESN'T HAVE AN ALIEN HERO TO BACK HIM UP!

WEAKNESSES

BEN TENDS TO RUSH INTO THINGS WITHOUT THINKING. HE'S A BIG SHOW-OFF AND LOVES THE ATTENTION THE OMNITRIX BRINGS HIM. HE'S ALSO BEEN KNOWN TO USE IT FOR PRANKS ...

THE OMNITRIX

Box of Trix

AFTER IT CRASH-LANDS ON EARTH, THE OMNITRIX ATTACHES ITSELF TO BEN'S WRIST - AND WON'T COME OFF! SINCE THERE'S NO INSTRUCTION MANUAL, BEN HAS TO WORK OUT HOW TO USE IT BY HIMSELF ...

WHAT IS IT?

THE OMNITRIX IS AN ADVANCED ALIEN DEVICE, WHICH ALLOWS THE WEARER TO TURN THEMSELVES INTO THE ALIEN OF THEIR CHOICE FOR A SHORT TIME.

DEFECTS

THE OMNITRIX DOESN'T ALWAYS TURN BEN INTO THE ALIEN HE WANTS, AND SOMETIMES REFUSES TO WORK AT ALL. IT ALSO TAKES TIME TO RECHARGE AFTER EACH TRANSFORMATION.

ENHANCEMENTS

AT FIRST, THE OMNITRIX GIVES BEN 10 ALIENS. BUT IT HAS MORE SECRET POWERS THAT HE WILL UNLOCK OVER TIME. JUST TURN THE PAGE TO FIND OUT HOW BEN FIRST DISCOVERED THE OMNITRIX ...

BEN 10™

AND THEN THERE WERE 10

BEN TENNYSON HAS JUST FINISHED SCHOOL FOR THE SUMMER. HE'S OFF ON A ROAD TRIP WITH HIS GRANDPA MAX IN THEIR OLD 'RV' – THE RUSTBUCKET! MEANWHILE, SOME VERY STRANGE THINGS ARE HAPPENING IN OUTER SPACE.

AN ALIEN SPACESHIP IS CRUISING SILENTLY THROUGH SPACE WHEN SUDDENLY, *BOOM!* A SMALLER SHIP DELIVERS A DEVASTATING BLAST OF ENERGY!

ZAP! POW! THE ATTACK CONTINUES, ROCKING THE BIGGER SPACE CRAFT.

ON BOARD THE DAMAGED SHIP IS THE MONSTROUS-LOOKING VILGAX, AN EVIL ALIEN WARLORD.

I HAVE COME TOO FAR TO BE DENIED.

THE OMNITRIX SHALL BE MINE, AND THERE IS NOT A BEING IN THE GALAXY WHO DARES STAND IN MY WAY!

THE SPACE CHASE CONTINUES ...

MEANWHILE, ON PLANET EARTH, BEN TENNYSON IS GETTING UP TO HIS USUAL PRANKS IN THE CLASSROOM. IT'S THE LAST DAY OF THE SCHOOL YEAR, AND HE CAN'T WAIT TO GET AWAY. THE CLOCK TURNS THREE.

YES! OUTTA HERE!

BEN'S HEADING OUT THE DOOR.

OUTSIDE, BEN'S GRANDPA MAX IS WAITING IN HIS RV.

COME ON BEN, LET'S GO.

WE'RE BURNING DAYLIGHT. I WANT TO MAKE IT TO THE CAMPSITE BY NIGHTFALL.

BEN CLIMBS ON BOARD THE RV. BUT HE IS IN FOR A BIG SHOCK!

WHAT IS **SHE** DOING HERE?

IT'S HIS COUSIN, GWEN.

TAKE IT EASY DWEEB, THIS WASN'T MY IDEA. SOMEONE CONVINCED MY MUM THAT GOING CAMPING FOR THE SUMMER WOULD BE GOOD FOR ME.

I THOUGHT IT WOULD BE FUN IF YOUR COUSIN JOINED US THIS SUMMER, IS THAT A PROBLEM?

"I CAN'T BELIEVE IT, I WAIT ALL SCHOOL YEAR TO GO ON THIS TRIP, AND NOW THE QUEEN OF COOTIES IS ALONG FOR THE RIDE!" MOANS BEN.

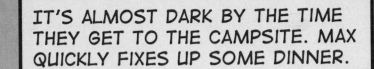

IT'S ALMOST DARK BY THE TIME THEY GET TO THE CAMPSITE. MAX QUICKLY FIXES UP SOME DINNER.

"CHOW TIME!" SAYS MAX. "MARINATED MEAL WORMS. IT'S HARD TO FIND THEM FRESH. THEY'RE A DELICACY IN SOME COUNTRIES."

AND TOTALLY GROSS IN OTHERS!

URGH, COULDN'T WE JUST HAVE A BURGER OR SOMETHING?

"IF THESE DON'T SOUND GOOD," CONTINUES MAX, "I'VE GOT SOME SMOKED SHEEP'S TONGUE IN THE FRIDGE ..."

BACK IN OUTER SPACE, THE FEROCIOUS BATTLE CONTINUES. VILGAX'S SPACESHIP ATTACKS THE SMALLER CRAFT AND MANAGES TO DESTROY ITS FORWARD-THRUSTING SYSTEM.

BANG!

PREPARE TO BOARD,

I WANT THE OMNITRIX **NOW!**

BUT THE SMALLER CRAFT FIRES ITS FINAL LASER BLAST AT VILGAX'S SHIP. **BANG!** THERE'S A HUGE EXPLOSION! VILGAX ISN'T BEATEN – HIS SPACESHIP ATTACKS, AND THE SMALL CRAFT BREAKS IN HALF.

WHOOSH!

A ROCKET-SHAPED OBJECT TUMBLES OUT AND HURTLES DOWN INTO THE DARKNESS, PLUMMETING TOWARDS EARTH ...

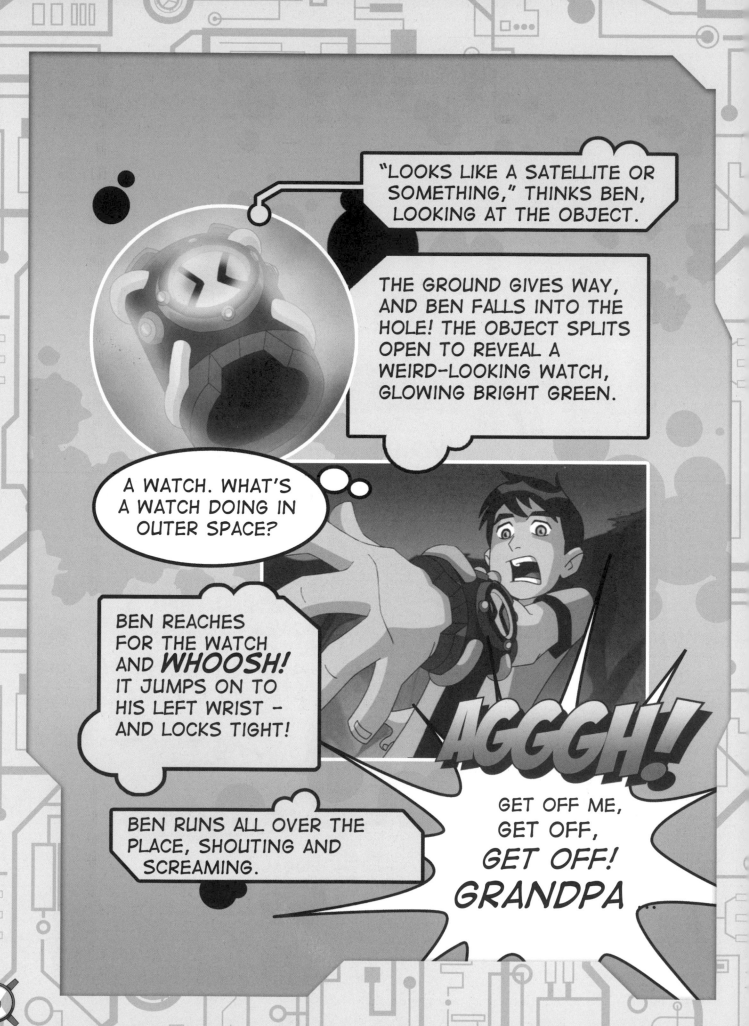

BACK IN THE FOREST, BEN PULLS HIMSELF OUT OF THE CRATER. HE TRIES AGAIN TO GET THE WATCH OFF, BUT NOTHING WORKS.

BEN TAKES A CLOSE LOOK AT THE WATCH AND PRESSES A BUTTON. IT POPS UP AND BLINKS GREEN. A PICTURE OF A MONSTER SUDDENLY APPEARS.

COOL!

BEN CAN'T RESIST PRESSING THE BUTTON.

... AND SUDDENLY BEN HAS TRANSFORMED INTO A BURNING MAN – *HEATBLAST!* HE RUNS THROUGH THE FOREST CRYING OUT IN TERROR.

AGGGH!

I'M ON FIRE, I'M ON FIRE ... HEY, I'M ON FIRE, AND I'M OK. CHECK IT OUT, *I'M TOTALLY HOT!*

BEN TRIES OUT HIS NEW POWERS – IT'S PRETTY COOL BEING ABLE TO SHOOT *FIREBALLS!* BUT IT ISN'T LONG BEFORE HE ACCIDENTALLY SETS FIRE TO SOME TREES. THE FIRE SPREADS AND SOON A HUGE FOREST FIRE IS RAGING! HEATBLAST PANICS.

JUST THEN, MAX AND GWEN APPEAR, ARMED WITH FIRE EXTINGUISHERS. BUT THEY DIDN'T RECKON ON FINDING BEN DISGUISED AS A MONSTER FIREBALL!

BACK IN SPACE, VILGAX IS RECOVERING IN A REGENERATION TANK ON HIS SHIP. THE EVIL WARLORD ANGRILY SHOUTS AT ONE OF HIS ROBOTIC ASSISTANTS ...

WHAT DO YOU MEAN IT'S NOT THERE? THIS BATTLE NEARLY COSTS ME MY LIFE AND YOU SAY THE OMNITRIX IS NO LONGER ON BOARD?

THE ROBOT REPORTS THAT "SENSORS INDICATE A PROBE WAS JETTISONED FROM THE SHIP JUST BEFORE BOARDING. IT LANDED ON THE PLANET BELOW."

GO! BRING IT TO ME!

BACK AT THE CAMP, MAX AND GWEN MANAGED TO SNUFF OUT THE FLAMES. HEATBLAST TELLS THEM ALL ABOUT THE WATCH AND WHAT JUST HAPPENED TO HIM.

THINK HE'S GONNA STAY A MONSTER FOREVER?

BEN'S AN ALIEN. I MEAN, LOOK AT HIM. WHAT ELSE COULD HE BE?

"I DON'T WANNA BE FIRE GUY FOREVER!"

"DON'T WORRY, BEN," SAYS MAX. "WE'LL FIGURE THIS THING OUT."

THE WATCH SUDDENLY *BLEEPS*, AND WITH A SMALL, BRIGHT EXPLOSION, HEATBLAST TURNS BACK INTO BEN!

MAX GOES TO EXPLORE THE CRATER, TELLING BEN AND GWEN TO STAY SAFE BY THE CAMP. BEN EXAMINES THE WATCH ...

"SO," SAYS GWEN, "WHAT DID IT FEEL LIKE GOING ALL ALIEN?"

IT FREAKED ME OUT AT FIRST. HEY, I THINK I FIGURED OUT HOW I DID IT. SHOULD I TRY IT AGAIN, JUST ONCE?

BEN PRESSES THE WATCH ... AND TRANSFORMS INTO A WILD, HAIRY, GROWLING, DROOLING BEAST.

IT'S *WILDMUTT!*

"YEUGH!" SAYS GWEN. "THIS THING'S EVEN UGLIER THAN YOU ARE NORMALLY! YOU NEED A FLEA COLLAR ON THIS MUTT! AND NO EYES? WHAT GOOD IS THIS ONE? IT CAN'T SEE!"

WILDMUTT MAY NOT HAVE EYES, BUT HIS RADAR-LIKE 'VISION' CAN DETECT PEOPLE AND OBJECTS AROUND HIM. HE BOUNDS OFF INTO THE FOREST, LEAPING AND SWINGING FROM TREE TO TREE ...

BEFORE LONG, WILDMUTT SENSES DANGER. A ROBOTIC DRONE FLIES TOWARDS HIM!

WILDMUTT JUMPS ON TOP OF THE DRONE. WITH HIS SHARP TEETH HE TEARS ITS WIRES OUT, AND THE DRONE SPINS WILDLY OUT OF CONTROL! WILDMUTT LEAPS OFF, SECONDS BEFORE THE MACHINE EXPLODES.

JUST THEN, WILDMUTT TURNS BACK INTO BEN. BAD TIMING! A SECOND DRONE IS HEADING STRAIGHT FOR BEN.

LUCKILY GWEN ARRIVES, AND SHE SMACKS THE DRONE HARD WITH A SPADE, AND DESTROYS IT. BEN IS IMPRESSED!

NEVER THOUGHT I'D SAY THIS, BUT AM I GLAD TO SEE YOU!

BEN AND GWEN RUN BACK TO THE CAMP TO FIND GRANDPA MAX.

BACK AT CAMP, THE TEAM HEAR A MAYDAY CALL OVER THE RUSTBUCKET'S RADIO – "MAYDAY, MAYDAY! SOMEBODY HELP US. WE'RE UNDER ATTACK BY SOME SORT OF … ROBOT!"

SOUNDS JUST LIKE THOSE THINGS THAT ATTACKED ME, THEY MUST BE LOOKING FOR THE WATCH. I THINK I CAN HELP!

WITH A PRESS OF THE BUTTON, BEN TRANSFORMS AGAIN, THIS TIME INTO A MAN TOUGHER THAN ANY METAL. IT'S *DIAMONDHEAD!*

"SO," SAYS GWEN, "WHAT CAN THIS GUY DO?"

I DUNNO, BUT I BET IT'S GONNA BE *COOL!*

DIAMONDHEAD, MAX AND GWEN ARRIVE AT THE SCENE OF THE ATTACK. VILGAX'S HUGE ROBOTIC ASSISTANT HAS LANDED ON EARTH TO CAPTURE THE OMNITRIX. HE'S FIRING WEAPONS, CAUSING EXPLOSIONS AND FIRES. CAMPERS ARE RUNNING FOR THEIR LIVES ...

"LOOKS LIKE PAPA ROBOT THIS TIME," SAYS DIAMONDHEAD. "I'LL GET GEARHEAD'S ATTENTION. YOU TWO GUYS GET THE CAMPERS TO SAFETY."

THE ROBOT IS FIERCE, BUT DIAMONDHEAD'S GLASS-LIKE SURFACE REFLECTS ITS LASERS BACK AT IT. FINALLY, THE ROBOT RIVAL IS DESTROYED!

BACK ON HIS SPACESHIP, THE INJURED VILGAX CANNOT BELIEVE THAT HIS DRONE HAS FAILED TO GET THE OMNITRIX.

AT THE CAMPSITE, MAX AND GWEN ARE PACKING UP, GETTING READY TO LEAVE. SUDDENLY A SUPER-SPEEDY ALIEN APPEARS. IT'S BEN AS XLR8! HE ZIPS AROUND AND HELPS PACK UP THE RUSTBUCKET. HE'S SO FAST!

NO!

"I THINK THIS IS GOING TO BE THE BEST SUMMER EVER!" LAUGHS XLR8.

"ABSOLUTELY!" AGREES MAX.

"IT'S DEFINITELY GOING TO BE INTERESTING ..." SAYS GWEN.

HOW TO DRAW BEN

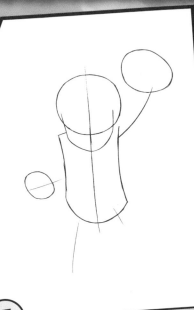

1 DRAW A CIRCLE WITH A SEMI-CIRCLE UNDERNEATH FOR BEN'S HEAD. ADD LINES FOR THE POSITION OF ARMS WITH CIRCLES FOR HANDS. DRAW BEN'S CHEST.

2 USING THE LINES AS A GUIDE, THICKEN UP THE ARMS. CREATE THE LEGS BY DRAWING LINES, THEN THICKEN THEM UP AND ADD SEMI-CIRCLES FOR FEET.

3 ADD HAIR, EARS AND EYES IN THE HEAD CIRCLE. USE THE SEMI-CIRCLE FOR HIS JAW AND MOUTH. CREATE A FIST IN THE HAND CIRCLES AND ADD BEN'S CLOTHES.

4 DRAW OVER BEN'S OUTLINE, LEAVING OUT ANY SKETCHY LINES. DON'T FORGET TO ADD HIS WATCH. COLOUR HIM IN AND HE'S ALL READY FOR ACTION!

Practise your Ben sketches on this page!

CHARACTER CLOSE-UP

GWEN TENNYSON

Voice of Reason

GWEN IS BEN'S COUSIN. SHE CAN'T UNDERSTAND WHY THE COOLEST GADGET IN THE GALAXY ENDED UP ON THE WRIST OF THE BIGGEST DWEEB IN THE GALAXY. BUT EVEN SHE HAS TO ADMIT THAT BEN DOES GOOD SOMETIMES ...

PERSONALITY

GWEN TRIES TO KEEP BEN FROM GOING TOO WILD. SHE THINKS AHEAD, AND TRIES TO STOP BEN GETTING INTO TROUBLE (USUALLY WITHOUT SUCCESS). SHE IS AS SENSIBLE AS BEN IS MISCHIEVOUS.

STRENGTHS

GWEN HAS A STRONG NATURAL TALENT FOR MAGIC – SHE'S GOOD WITH MAGICAL OBJECTS AND SPELLS. SHE ALSO HAS MARTIAL ARTS SKILLS, AND SHE'S HANDY WITH MACHINES.

WEAKNESSES

GWEN HAS A TENDENCY TO THINK SHE'S RIGHT ALL THE TIME. EVEN WHEN SHE IS, IT'S PRETTY ANNOYING! SHE ALSO GETS JEALOUS WHEN BEN HOGS ALL THE ATTENTION.

ALIEN MAZE

Gwen needs to get to Ben! The bad guys have trapped him in a corner. Guide Gwen through the maze, so she can help Ben kick some butt! Make sure you avoid the bad guys.

Found the way? Cool!
Now it's time to kick serious butt!

CHECK YOUR ANSWER ON PAGE 254.

WHAT HAPPENS NEXT?

Look at these scenes from the awesome Ben 10 show. Write what you think is happening, and how you think things turn out in the end. You can make up different stories and endings!

MAX TENNYSON

Adventurous Senior

MAX IS BEN AND GWEN'S 60-YEAR-OLD GRANDPA. HE CAN'T WAIT TO TAKE THEM ON A SUMMER ADVENTURE IN HIS MOTORHOME. BUT HE HAS NO IDEA WHAT AN ADVENTURE IT WILL BE ...

PERSONALITY

MAX HAS A REAL TASTE FOR ADVENTURE, AND WANTS BEN AND GWEN TO SHARE IN THE FUN. HE ALSO HAS A TASTE FOR WEIRD FOOD – SOMETHING THEY AREN'T SO KEEN TO SHARE!

STRENGTHS

MAX HAS A GOOD KNOWLEDGE OF ALIENS, WEAPONS AND TECHNOLOGY – IN FACT, A SUSPICIOUSLY GOOD KNOWLEDGE, SEEING AS HE CLAIMS HE USED TO BE A PLUMBER ...

WEAKNESSES

IS MAX HIDING SOMETHING FROM HIS GRANDKIDS? THERE'S DEFINITELY SOMETHING ABOUT HIS PAST THAT DOESN'T ADD UP, AND BEN AND GWEN WANT TO KNOW THE TRUTH.

RUNAWAY RUSTBUCKET

Max needs to get to the Rustbucket – and fast! Help Max find the right path to the Rustbucket before it's too late.

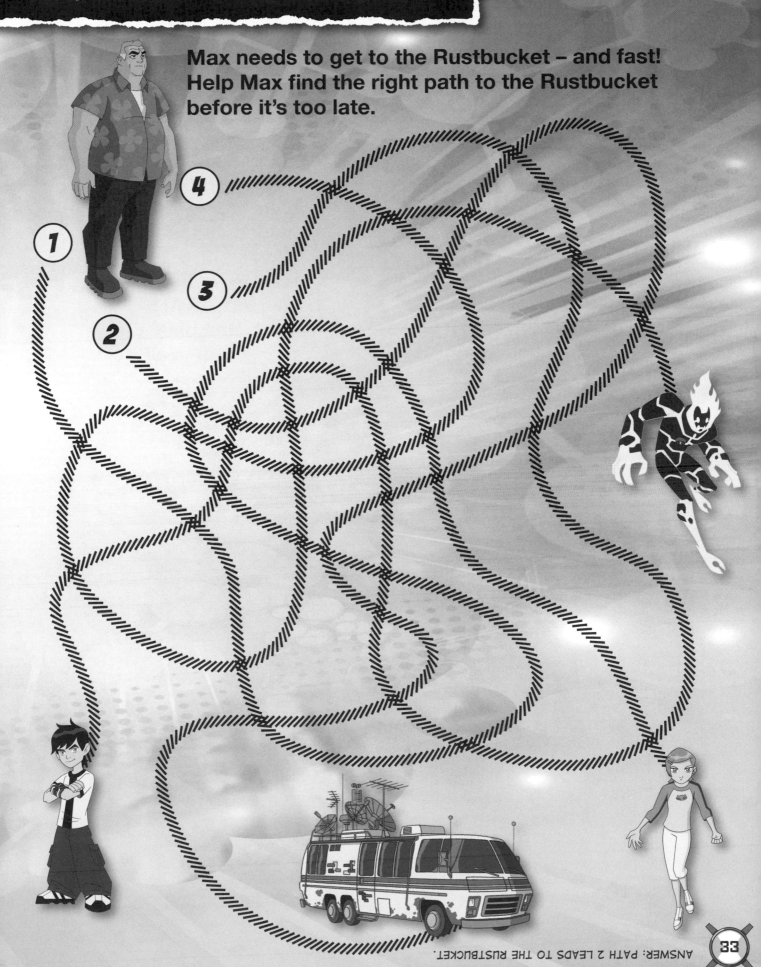

ANSWER: PATH 2 LEADS TO THE RUSTBUCKET.

HEATBLAST

When Ben changes into Heatblast he can aim bolts of fire from his hands and mouth. He can also create fireballs for weapons. When angry, Heatblast can throw heat in all directions.

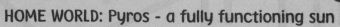

HOME WORLD: Pyros - a fully functioning sun

SPECIES: Pyronite

APPEARANCE: has fire coming out from his body

STRENGTHS: fire-resistant body, and can control flames and heat

WEAKNESSES: vulnerable to water; he can also burn things without meaning to

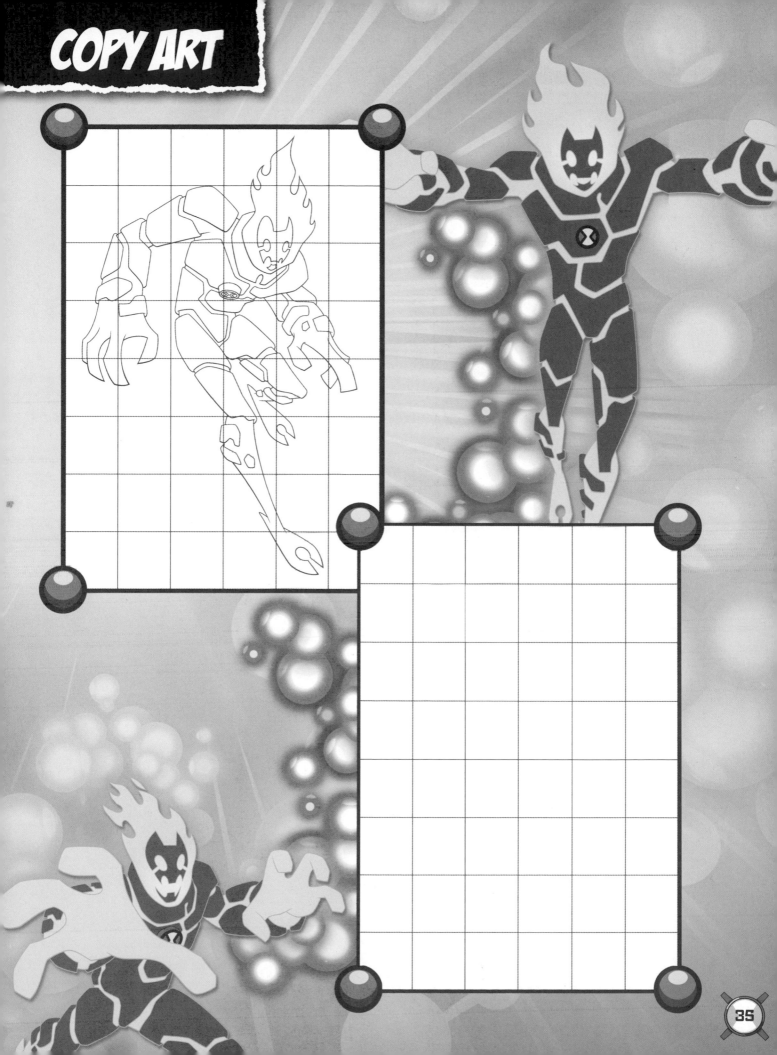

TO THE RESCUE

GWEN'S IN TROUBLE! YOU NEED TO GET TO HER FAST. STARTING FROM GRANDPA, PASS THROUGH EACH ALIEN ONCE, IN THE DIRECTION OF THE ARROW. YOU CAN GO THROUGH THE ROBOT DRONES, BUT YOU CAN'T GO DOWN THE SAME PATH TWICE.

ALIEN   DRONE

BEN's TIP
TRY DOING IT IN PENCIL FIRST!

YOU FOUND GWEN. BUT NOW THE OMNITRIX IS OUT OF JUICE! YOU NEED TO GET BACK TO GRANDPA, AVOIDING ALL THE ROBOT DRONES (DON'T WORRY ABOUT THE ALIENS OR ARROWS THIS TIME!).

FOUR ARMS

Ben transforms into Four Arms whenever he needs an extra pair of hands! He has armour-plated skin and big muscles. He has incredibly strong legs, and he can leap great distances.

HOME WORLD: Khoros - a dusty and cruel place

SPECIES: Tetramand

APPEARANCE: huge - he's 4 metres tall - with four arms and armoured skin

STRENGTHS: great at throwing and smashing things

WEAKNESSES: can be clumsy - not good in small places

WASHOUT

BEN WANTED TO GO HEATBLAST TO PUT OUT A FIRE, BUT HE GOT FOUR ARMS INSTEAD! NEVER MIND – IF HE PULLS DOWN A WATER TOWER, THE DRY RIVER BEDS WILL LEAD THE WATER TO THE FLAMES. BUT WHICH WATER TOWER WILL PUT OUT ALL THE FIRES? (REMEMBER, WATER ONLY FLOWS DOWNHILL – DUH!)

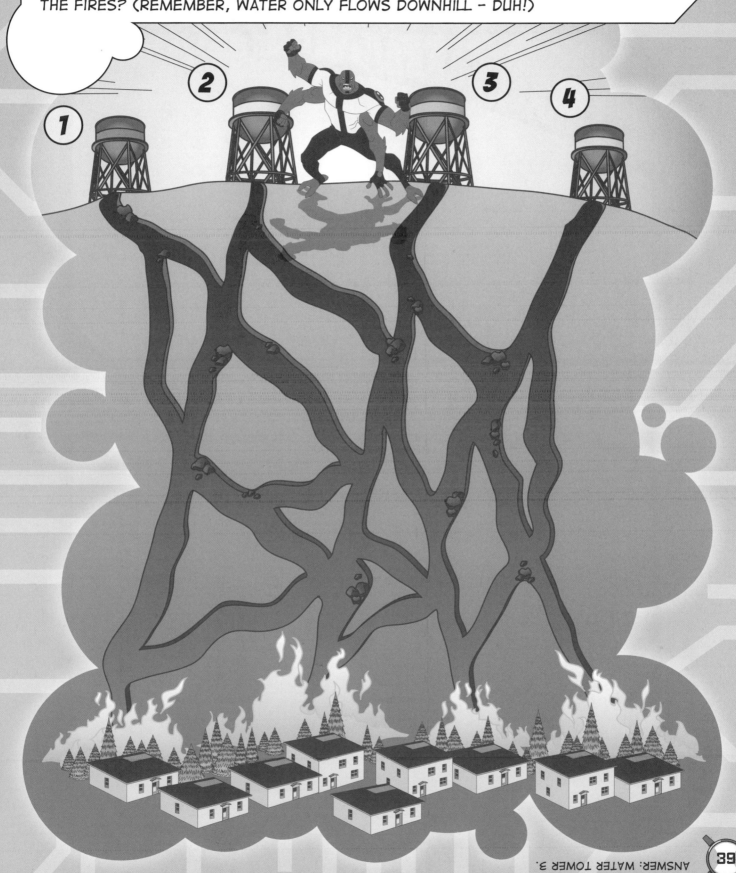

ANSWER: WATER TOWER 3.

HERO TIME!

Read the story, then draw pictures and use your stickers to make your own cartoon strip!

RRAAAAAAAAAAAAAAAAA!

BEN IS PLAYING ON HIS SKATEBOARD, WHEN HE HEARS A TERRIFYING NOISE.

IT'S EVIL VILGAX – AND HE WANTS BEN'S OMNITRIX!

BEN TRANSFORMS INTO FOUR ARMS. "WATCH OUT OLD GUY, I'M GONNA KICK SOME BUTT!"

FOUR ARMS WINS THE BATTLE AND VILGAX RUNS BACK TO HIS SPACESHIP. BEN IS SAFE ... FOR NOW.

STINKFLY

Ben turns into Stinkfly whenever he needs to fly. He has pincers and a sharp tail, and hard spikes on his forearms. Stinkfly can produce dangerous chemicals from the plants he eats.

HOME WORLD: Lepidopterra - a peaceful swamp planet

SPECIES: Lepidopterran

APPEARANCE: an insectoid alien with wings, sharp pincers and pointed tail

STRENGTHS: can fly; is acrobatic and intelligent

WEAKNESSES: poisonous chemicals and gas can harm him, and slow him down

STORMFRONT

GETTING TO THE ISLAND OUT AT SEA WOULD HAVE BEEN A BREEZE WITH RIPJAWS. UNFORTUNATELY, BEN WENT STINKFLY – AND THERE'S A STORM BREWING! WHERE SHOULD BEN TAKE OFF SO THE STRONG WINDS BLOW HIM TO THE ISLAND? STARTING AT THE DIFFERENT PLACES, MOVE THE NUMBER SHOWN IN THE DIRECTION OF THE ARROW TO SEE IF YOU REACH THE ISLAND.

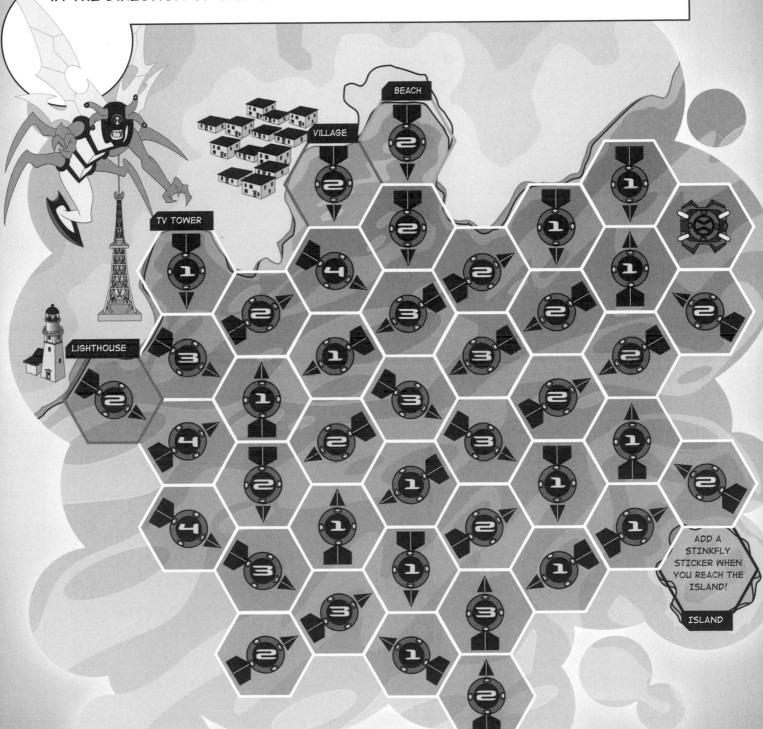

ADD A STINKFLY STICKER WHEN YOU REACH THE ISLAND!

ANSWER: BEN MUST LAUNCH FROM THE TV TOWER.

BEN 10 BLAST FROM THE PAST

SHOLLY FISCH
WRITER

ETHEN BEAVERS
PENCILLER

MIKE DECARLO
INKER

JOHN J. HILL
LETTERER

HEROIC AGE
COLORIST

RACHEL GLUCKSTERN
ASSOC. EDITOR

JOAN HILTY
EDITOR

BEN 10 CREATED BY
MAN OF ACTION

GRANDPA MAX? ARE YOU SERIOUS?

TIME HAS NOT DIMMED MY MEMORY, BOY.

"YEARS AGO, MAXWELL TENNYSON WAS PART OF YOUR WORLD'S SECRET DEFENSE FORCE, THE PLUMBERS! HE AND HIS PARTNER EXILED US FROM THIS BACKWATER PLANET!"

BUT NOW, WE HAVE RETURNED--

--FOR REVENGE!

OH, YEAH? NOT IF I--

NO, BEN. I'LL HANDLE THIS!

HUH? BUT, GRANDPA, THERE'S THREE OF THEM-- AND THEY'VE GOT GUNS!

MAYBE YOU BEAT THESE GUYS BACK IN THE DAY, BUT NOW...

"NOW" WHAT? I'M TOO OLD?!

I SAID I'LL HANDLE THIS.

YOU TAKE COVER! GO!

NO, SLEZAK. DON'T WASTE YOUR *AMMUNITION.*

THE ONE *WE* WANT IS TENNYSON!

WHAT'RE YOU *DOING,* TWERP? YOU'RE NOT GOING TO *HELP* GRANDPA?

WHAT DO YOU *WANT* FROM ME? HE TOLD ME *NOT* TO!

YOU'RE GOING TO LET YOUR GRANDFATHER GET *KILLED* BY HEAVILY ARMED *SUPER-ALIENS*--

--JUST SO HE DOESN'T FEEL *OLD?*

NO WAY! DON'T BE A DWEEB!

BUT WHAT GRANDPA DOESN'T *KNOW* WON'T *HURT* HIM.

SO NOW THAT WE'RE *OUT* OF SIGHT--

--IT'S TIME TO *GET SMALL*--

--AS *GREY MATTER!*

REMEMBER ME?

I'LL JUST HAVE TO DO THIS WITH MY *BARE HANDS!*

SHEESH! IT'S LIKE THIS GUY SWALLOWED THE *"IDIOT'S GUIDE TO SUPER-VILLAIN DIALOGUE"* OR SOMETHING!

WELL, MAYBE THIS ¿NNGH¿ *SKI POLE* WILL SHUT HIM UP.

WHUMMPF!

KRROWWW

WATCH YOUR STEP, HONCH--

--THAT SNOW IS *SLIPPERY!*

HA! YOU *MISSED!*

GRANDPA! GRANDPA! ARE YOU OKAY?

'COURSE I AM, GWEN.

THOSE ARE THE GUYS YOU SHOULD BE ASKING ABOUT.

I'LL CALL SOMEONE TO PICK UP THE *TRASH.*

WHOA! ALIENS ON ICE!

GRANDPA-- YOU BEAT THESE GUYS ALL BY *YOURSELF?*

FEELS *GOOD* TO KNOW THE OLD MAN'S STILL *GOT* IT, HUH?

BUT YOU KNOW WHAT'S EVEN *BETTER?*

KNOWING I'VE GOT FAMILY THAT *CARES* ENOUGH TO WATCH MY BACK--

--WITHOUT HURTING MY FOOLISH *PRIDE.*

UH...

WE WERE JUST...

I KNOW. THANKS, KIDS.

ANYTIME, GRANDPA.

ANYTIME.

the END

YOUR OWN ALIEN

If you had the choice - what kind of alien would you create?
Choose some alien features from the lists below, and design
your own cool alien dude. Then draw it on the next page.

Size
- ☐ Very big
- ☐ Medium
- ☐ Very small

Strength
- ☐ Very strong
- ☐ Medium strength
- ☐ Not very strong

Colour
- ☐ Red
- ☐ Blue
- ☐ Green
- ☐ Black
- ☐ Grey
- ☐ Orange
- ☐ Purple
- ☐ Yellow
- ☐ White
- ☐ Brown

Skin type
- ☐ Slimy
- ☐ Rough and bumpy
- ☐ Smooth and shiny

Special Features
- ☐ Fast
- ☐ Can fly
- ☐ Technical
- ☐ Can swim
- ☐ Intelligent

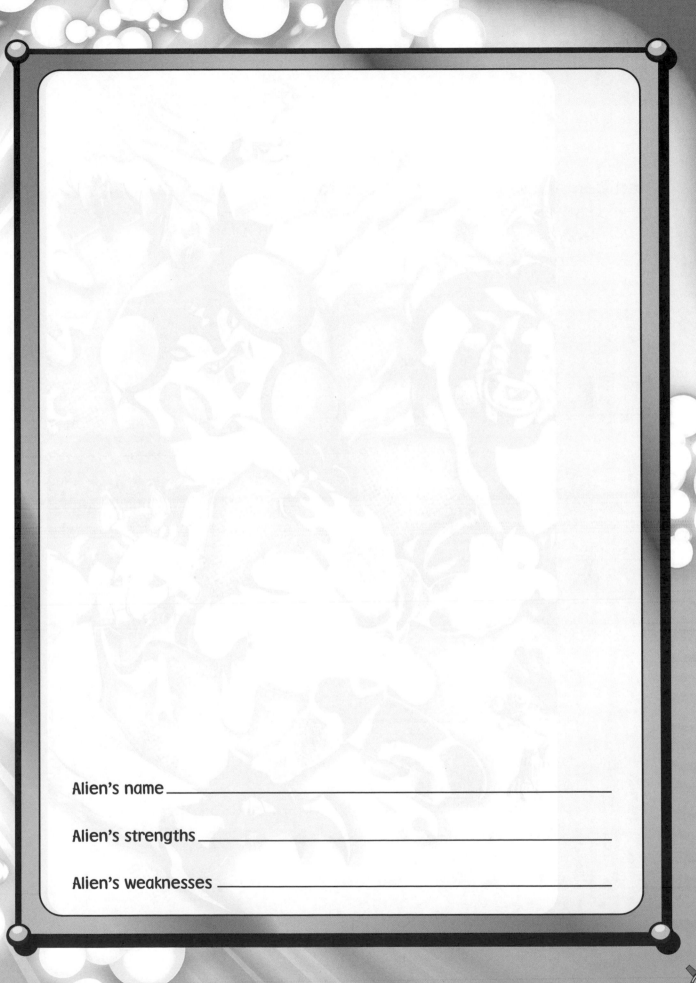

Alien's name _____

Alien's strengths _____

Alien's weaknesses _____

WILDMUTT

When Ben needs to be vicious and fast, Wildmutt is the guy. A cross between a lion and a gorilla, he has spiky quills on his back which act as finely-tuned sensors, so few things escape Wildmutt's radar-like 'sight'.

HOME WORLD: Vulpin - a toxic, dark planet
SPECIES: Vulpimancer
APPEARANCE: a blind beast with powerful, apelike arms
STRENGTHS: ferocious and quick, with strong sense of smell, hearing and taste
WEAKNESSES: cannot see or talk, and is sensitive to loud noises and strong smells

GHOSTFREAK

Ben becomes Ghostfreak and sometimes even spooks himself! Ghostfreak has a single eye, and exposed bones on certain parts of his body. He floats above the ground and can fire energy blasts from his chest. It is thought he can mind-read.

HOME WORLD: Anur Phaetos - a dark, mysterious world

SPECIES: Ectonurite

APPEARANCE: a ghost-like, shadowy alien

STRENGTHS: can drift through walls, become invisible and 'possess' people

WEAKNESSES: intense, prolonged light (and chemicals) can damage him

ALIEN ART

HERE'S AN ACE BEN 10 ACTION SCENE FOR YOU TO COLOUR IN! USE ALL SORTS OF COLOURS TO FINISH THE PICTURE, AND SEE HOW FAST YOU CAN COMPLETE IT!

NOW USE YOUR STICKERS TO CREATE
YOUR OWN BEN 10 POSTER!

WHERE'S BEN?

How many times can you find Ben in this grid? Read forwards, backwards, up, down and diagonally.

B	N	E	E	B	B	E	N
B	E	N	B	N	N	E	E
B	N	E	B	B	N	E	E
N	B	B	N	E	E	N	E
N	E	B	N	N	B	B	E
B	N	E	E	B	E	N	N
B	N	B	E	B	B	E	N
B	E	E	N	N	B	N	E

CHECK YOUR ANSWERS ON PAGE 254.

RIPJAWS

Whenever Ben needs to be fierce under water, he becomes Ripjaws. Covered in scales, he can turn his legs into a large tail with claw-tipped fins. His sharp teeth can bite through almost anything.

HOME WORLD: Piscciss - a dangerous underwater world
SPECIES: Piscciss Volanns
APPEARANCE: a mix of alligator, leech and eel
STRENGTHS: a powerful and fast swimmer, with razor-sharp teeth
WEAKNESSES: is useless above water

GREY MATTER

When Ben needs an intelligence boost, he'll turn into Grey Matter. The little alien is able to enter complex machines and operate them from the inside.

HOME WORLD: Galvan Prime - a scientifically advanced world
SPECIES: Galvan
APPEARANCE: very small (height: 13 cm), with slimy skin and sharp teeth
STRENGTHS: incredibly intelligent and highly technical
WEAKNESSES: he is not built for combat

VILGAX HUNT

GREY MATTER IS LOOKING FOR VILGAX. THE DOT ON THE GRID BELOW SHOWS WHERE THE EVIL WARLORD WAS LAST DETECTED. FOLLOW THE INSTRUCTIONS TO FIND THE COORDINATES OF WHERE VILGAX IS NOW. USE THE COMPASS TO HELP YOU. PLACE A STICKER OF GREY MATTER ON THE SPOT WHEN YOU'VE WORKED IT OUT!

FROM THE DOT, GO:
3 SQUARES EAST
2 SQUARES NORTH
1 SQUARE WEST

ANSWER: VILGAX IS IN BLOCK C2.

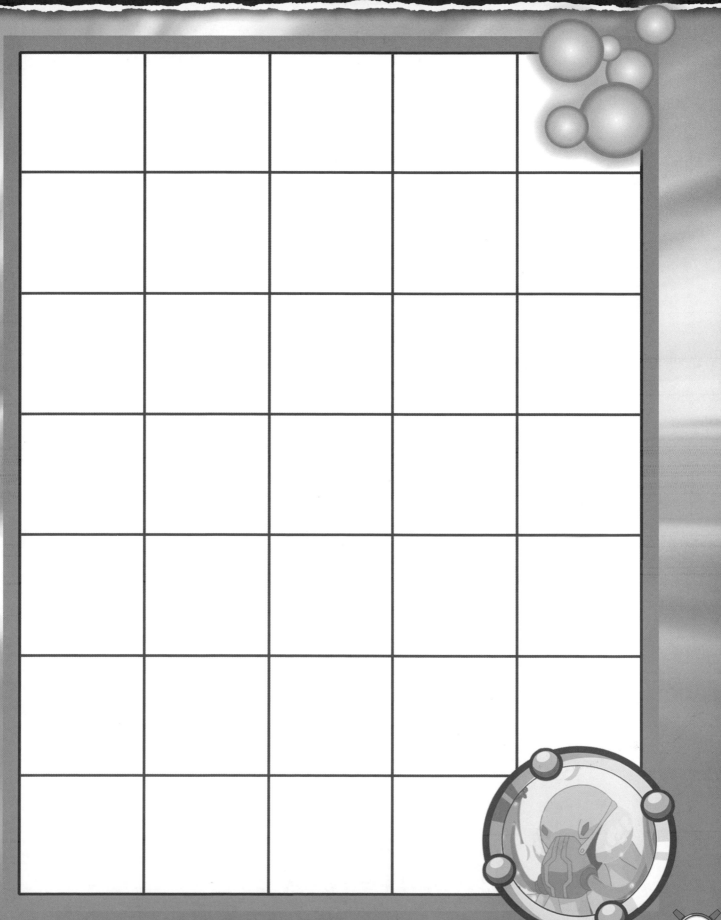

XLR8

Ben becomes XLR8 whenever he needs to be as fast as lightning. His amazing speed enables him to run up sheer walls and across non-solid ground such as mud, ice and water.

HOME WORLD: Kinet - a world of violent electrical storms
SPECIES: Kineceleran
APPEARANCE: blue skin, pointed features and large feet
STRENGTHS: can reach speeds of up to 300 miles per hour
WEAKNESSES: not built for fighting, and can be affected by magnets and electricity

THE REAL XLR8

XLR8 IS A SUPER-SPEEDY ALIEN! HOW LONG WILL IT TAKE YOU TO SPOT THE 5 DIFFERENCES BETWEEN PICTURES 1 AND 2? ON YOUR MARKS ...

ANSWERS: XLR8 IN PICTURE 2 IS MISSING THE OMNITRIX SYMBOL, HIS RIGHT CLAW, PART OF LEFT FOOT, AND HE HAS A LARGER WHITE STRIPE ON HIS CHEST, AND AN EXTRA STRIPE ON HIS TAIL.

DIAMONDHEAD

Ben becomes Diamondhead when he needs as much protection as possible from physical attack. This alien is able to cut and slash through almost anything. He can fire crystal shards from his body, and he can even re-grow lost limbs.

HOME WORLD: Petropia - a craggy, crystal-covered world

SPECIES: Petrosapien

APPEARANCE: razor-sharp crystals jut out from his body

STRENGTHS: his body is tougher than diamond, able to resist any light and beam-based weapons

WEAKNESSES: strong sonic vibrations can shatter his body

FIT 'EM IN!

FIT THESE ALIEN WORDS INTO THE GRID. THEN REARRANGE THE LETTERS IN THE SHADED BOXES TO MAKE A WORD THAT GWEN MIGHT THINK SHOULD HAVE BEEN ON THE LIST …

- ☐ UP
- ☐ FLY
- ☐ RIP
- ☐ ARMS
- ☐ FOUR
- ☐ GREY
- ☐ HEAD
- ☐ HEAT
- ☐ JAWS
- ☐ MUTT
- ☐ WILD
- ☐ XLR8
- ☐ BLAST
- ☐ FREAK
- ☐ GHOST
- ☐ GRADE
- ☐ STINK
- ☐ MATTER
- ☐ DIAMOND

WRITE THE WORD IN HERE!

WORD WARP

HOW MANY WORDS CAN YOU MAKE OUT OF THE LETTERS OF DIAMONDHEAD? NO POINTS FOR *DIAMOND* OR *HEAD!*

write the words here:

HOW MANY DID YOU GET?

GIVE YOURSELF 5 POINTS FOR OVER 5 WORDS, 10 POINTS FOR OVER 10 WORDS AND SO ON!

UPGRADE

If Ben wants to improve or transform any machinery, he'll turn into Upgrade. Upgrade is able to merge into metals and machines and can travel along wires.

HOME WORLD: Galvan B - a moon accidentally brought to life

SPECIES: Galvanic Mechomorphs

APPEARANCE: skin made from liquid metal, and has a single eye

STRENGTHS: can merge with any mechanical device and 'upgrade' it, and can fire a plasma beam from his eye

WEAKNESSES: electrical attacks and metal corrosives can harm him

MACHINE MERGE

Upgrade's skin is made from liquid metal, which allows him to merge with machinery. If you were Upgrade, what machines would you merge with? Maybe a bike, or a car, or even a spaceship? Draw a picture.

SPACE CAMP AND BEYOND

ROBBIE BUSCH
Writer

ETHEN BEAVERS
Penciller

MIKE DECARLO
Inker

MIKE SELLERS
Letterer

HEROIC AGE
Colorist

RACHEL GLUCKSTERN
Assoc. Editor

JOAN HILTY
Editor

BEN 10 created by **MAN OF ACTION**

OF COURSE I'M KIDDING! HA HA HA!

GO SUIT UP, PILOTS!

RAD! THANKS, GRANDPA!

YEAH! AND THANKS, GENERAL HOUSTON, THIS IS A DREAM COME TRUE!

LOOKS LIKE WE'VE GOT SOME NEW RECRUITS ON DECK! JUST SIT BACK AND ENJOY THE RIDE!

I'D REALLY LIKE TO HELP WITH SOMETHING. I'M PRETTY GOOD WITH COMPUTERS, CAPTAIN.

PRETTY GOOD? SHE'S A WHIZ!

YOU CAN CALL ME LEO.

UH... OKAY... SO WHERE DO I START?

HEY, I'M PATRICK AND THIS IS MY SISTER LORI. THAT'S RODNEY; HE'S LOST IN HIS OWN LITTLE WORLD.

HI, I'M BEN.

YOU GUYS ARE PRETTY LUCKY! THEY DON'T USUALLY LET KIDS WHO HAVEN'T TRAINED GO ON THESE SIMULATED MISSIONS.

WE'VE HAD SOME, UH, INTERGALACTIC EXPERIENCE.

HA!

SO, GWEN, YOU CAN HELP RODNEY.

HI. SO WHAT ARE YOU RUNNING? I'M UP ON THE LATEST OPERATING SYSTEM.

THIS ONE'S A LITTLE MORE ADVANCED. TRUST ME.

SHE'S HERE TO HELP. THAT'S AN ORDER, RODNEY.

YES, "CAPTAIN." SHE'LL BE A BIG HELP, I'M SURE.

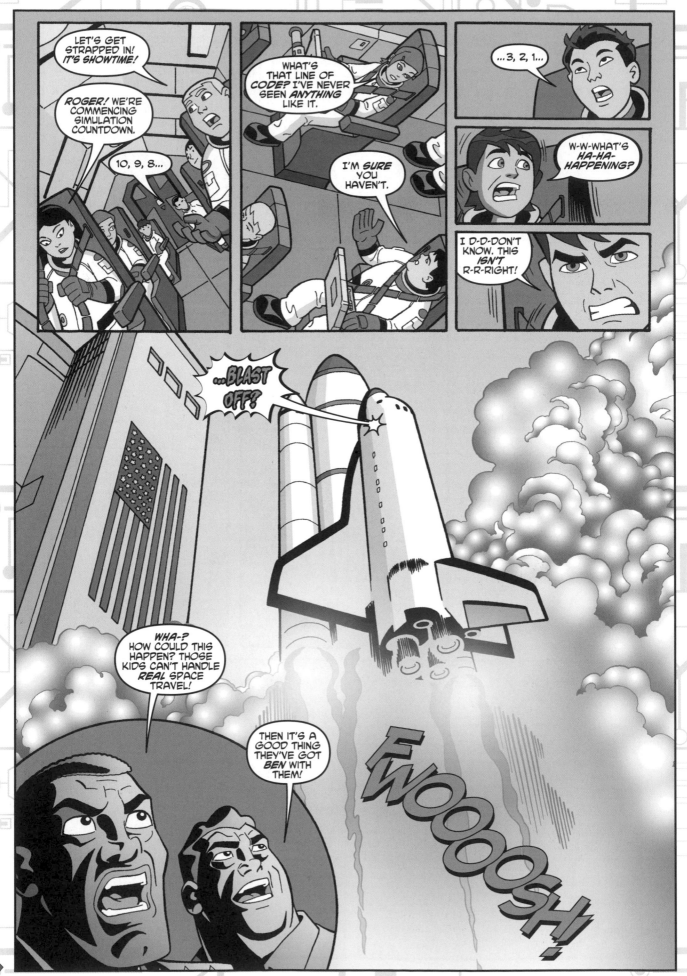

BEN? HE'S A NICE KID, BUT HE *BARELY* FILLS OUT THE SPACE SUIT.

YOU ALWAYS TOLD ME IT'S NOT THE *SUIT* THAT MAKES THE *MAN*.

FWOOP!

UH... GENERAL HOUSTON... WE HAVE A *PROBLEM!*

HOLY SMOKES! MAX, I TRULY HOPE YOU'RE *RIGHT* ABOUT THAT BOY.

ME TOO.

WHERE *ARE* WE?

WHERE ARE THE *STARS?* WE *BLASTED OFF,* RIGHT?

WE DID, BUT THEN SOMETHING *ELSE* HAPPENED.

I THINK IT'S TIME FOR A LITTLE *YOU-KNOW-WHAT.*

YEAH. I'M ON IT.

IT'S TIME TO *UPGRADE* OUR TRAVEL ARRANGEMENTS!

GWEN, ARE YOU OKAY?

OH MY GOSH! WHERE *IS* BEN?

HE'S OKAY... HE WAS JUST HERE... HE'LL *BE BACK.*

IS HE MESSING WITH THE COMPUTER SOMEWHERE? HE'LL MESH EVERYTHING UP! DOES HE HAVE A *PDA* OR SOMETHING?

OR *SOMETHING.*

WHAT ARE YOU *DOING?* IS THAT *ALIEN* CODE?

AND WHAT IF IT IS?

I NEED AN *ESCAPE ROUTE!* BUT THESE ALIEN CODES ARE RUNNING MY *SYSTEM* IN CIRCLES! I CAN'T THINK STRAIGHT!

I'M SURE EVEN *ALIEN* SYSTEMS REACT THE SAME WAY TO THE *ESCAPE* BUTTON!

NOOOO! YOU *STUPID* IDIOT!

HEY!

DON'T WORRY. WE'LL GET OUT OF HERE. *RIGHT,* RODNEY?

PATRICK! I DON'T LIKE THIS!

OKAY, *MEGA GEEK!* 'FESS UP! WHAT HAVE YOU *DONE?*

I HAVE BEEN *CHOSEN.* THE ALIENS WILL LEARN ENOUGH FROM US KIDS TO *RULE THE EARTH* WITH ME AS THEIR HUMAN EMPEROR!

HA! THOSE ALIENS WILL EAT YOU UP FOR BREAKFAST!

WHA--?

WHERE *WERE* YOU?

BEN! YOU'RE SAFE!

HE WAS CHECKING OUT THE...*UH...* SYSTEM... IN THE *CRAWL SPACE.* WHAT DID YOU FIND, BEN?

I FOUND *THIS* SYMBOL EVERYWHERE! AND I THINK IT CAN GET US *HOME!*

YOU'LL NEVER *DECIPHER* IT IN TIME. THE ALIENS ARE ON THEIR WAY *HERE* TO PICK US UP. IT'S *OVER* FOR YOU!

RODNEY, YOU HAVE *PASSED* OUR TEST. BUT WE NEED TO CHANGE THE *PLAN*. PSSS... TFFF... SSSSPPP...

YES, OF COURSE. I UNDERSTAND!

TAP INTO THE *FAIL-SAFE* SYSTEM AND *PROVE* YOUR WORTH WHILE I WORK FROM THE *INSIDE*.

I WILL NOT *DISAPPOINT* YOU!

WHEEE! *NOW* I SEE HOW THIS ALIEN CODE WORKS! LET'S TAKE IT ON HOME!

KRA-FOOOM!

UH-OH! BEN!

WHERE *IS* BEN?

DON'T WORRY; THEY SAID THEY HAD A *SPECIAL* MISSION FOR BEN BEFORE THEY SAID GOODBYE!

MISSION *ACCOMPLISHED!* LOOKS LIKE I'M RIGHT ON TIME!

‹HUH? STUPID HUMANS!›

PWOOP

CHOMP

I *KNEW* YOU TWO COULD GET THE KIDS SAFELY BACK TO OUR HOME DIMENSION!

ALL IT TOOK WAS A LITTLE BIT OF THE OLD *GREY MATTER.*

YEAH, WE POPPED BACK JUST IN TIME!

THE END

ALIEN RIDDLE

Fill in the letters, then add a sticker to show the answer.

MY FIRST IS IN ONE BUT NEVER IN NINE

MY SECOND'S IN MY AND ALSO IN MINE

MY THIRD IS IN NONSENSE AND ALSO IN FUN

MY FOURTH IS IN DID BUT IT'S NEVER IN DONE

MY FIFTH IS THE START AND THE END OF THIS HINT

MY SIXTH COMES JUST ONCE IN BOTH PAPER AND PRINT

MY SEVENTH'S IN MOIST BUT IT'S NOT IN THE MOSS

MY EIGHTH IS A RAY, AND IT LOOKS LIKE A CROSS.

ANSWER: OMNITRIX.

The Daily News

ALL-OUT ALIEN BATTLE TAKES OVER NEW YORK!

From the Alien Security Desk -
This picture was taken during a recent
disturbance involving the Security
~~~~~~~~~~ ~~~~~ beings

New York City at approximately 3.27pm
yesterday afternoon. As residents ran to
take cover, cars were overturned and fire
hydrants smashed as water gushed out
~~~~~~~~~~~~~~~ ~oaking the streets and

READY TO MEET SOME OF THE BAD GUYS?

VILGAX

WHO IS HE?
A vicious alien warlord and Ben's most powerful enemy.

APPEARANCE
Huge, with veiny arms and legs and an octopus-like head.

HIS AIM?
To steal the Omnitrix and rule the galaxy!

DR. ANIMO

WHO IS HE?
A researcher in veterinary science, who can transform animals into more dangerous versions of themselves.

APPEARANCE
An old man, with long grey hair and greenish skin.

HIS AIM?
To take over the world!

KEVIN 11

WHO IS HE?
A reckless teenager with absorbing powers.

APPEARANCE
Human with dark hair and clothes.

HIS AIM?
To cause mass devastation!

LIMAX

WHO ARE THEY?
Shape-shifting aliens from an unknown planet.

APPEARANCE
See-through green slime.

THEIR AIM?
To possess people and take them back to their planet!

HEX

WHO IS HE?
A magician with powers of witchcraft.

APPEARANCE
Tall and terrifying with pale skin.

HIS AIM?
To use his charms to control the world!

ZOMBOZO

WHO IS HE?
An evil clown.

APPEARANCE
Sickly blue skin and red hair.

HIS AIM?
To steal people's happiness!

SUPERHEROES YOU KNOW

Look at the list of strengths below. Many of Ben 10's aliens have some of these. See if you can find two of these strengths in each of your friends. Note them down in the spaces opposite.

Practical
Strong
Acrobatic
Energetic
Kind
Mischievous
Fast swimmer
Caring
Fast runner
Protective
Trustworthy
Funny
Technical
Intelligent

NAME: ....

STRENGTHS: ....

NAME: ....

STRENGTHS: ....

NAME: ....

STRENGTHS: ....

NAME: ....

STRENGTHS: ....

NAME: ....

STRENGTHS: ....

ALIEN POWER

Create your own super alien and draw it in the space below. Remember to give it a name and think up 3 awesome alien facts!

NAME: _____

SUPERPOWER: _____

STRENGTHS: _____

WEAKNESSES: _____

LAUNCH PAD!

Now create an awesome spaceship to bring your alien to Earth!

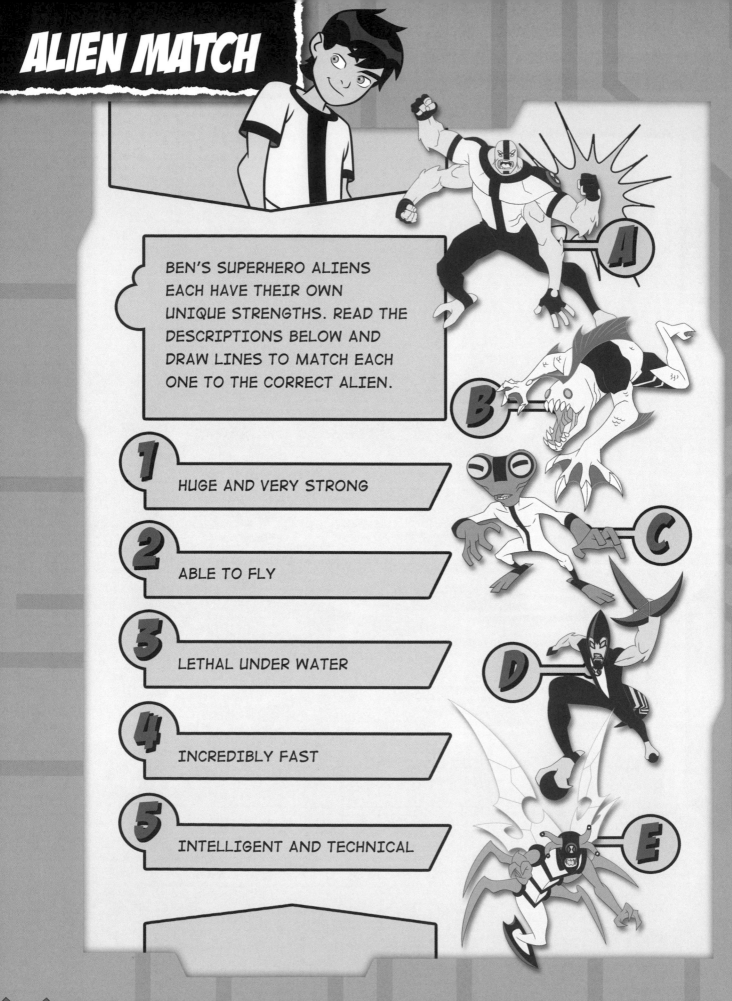

ALIEN MATCH

BEN'S SUPERHERO ALIENS EACH HAVE THEIR OWN UNIQUE STRENGTHS. READ THE DESCRIPTIONS BELOW AND DRAW LINES TO MATCH EACH ONE TO THE CORRECT ALIEN.

1 HUGE AND VERY STRONG

2 ABLE TO FLY

3 LETHAL UNDER WATER

4 INCREDIBLY FAST

5 INTELLIGENT AND TECHNICAL

ANSWERS: 1-A, 2-E, 3-B, 4-D, 5-C.

CODE BREAKER

GREY MATTER HAS INTERCEPTED A CODED MESSAGE FROM VILGAX. USE THE CODEBREAKER BELOW TO READ WHAT IT SAYS.

20 8 5   15 13 14 9 20 18 9 24   9 19

15 14   16 12 1 14 5 20   5 1 18 20 8

A	B	C	D	E	F	G	H	I	J
1	2	3	4	5	6	7	8	9	10
K	L	M	N	O	P	Q	R	S	T
11	12	13	14	15	16	17	18	19	20
	U	V	W	X	Y	Z			
	21	22	23	24	25	26			

AT LAST! I *FOUND* YOU -- -- YOU *ALIEN!*

WHO IN THE --?!

WHOA, DUDE -- *CHILL!* WE'VE GOT THE ALIEN *TIED UP!*

I BELIEVE

THE GUY IN THE CHAIR? *HE'S* NO ALIEN! I'M TALKING ABOUT *HIM!*

ME? AN *ALIEN?!* YOU'RE *CRAZY!*

YEAH, THAT'S WHAT YOU *WANT* PEOPLE TO THINK!

THAT'S WHY YOU ACCUSE *INNOCENT* PEOPLE -- TO DISTRACT ATTENTION FROM *YOU!*

WHAT ARE YOU EVEN *DOING* HERE? GET *OUT!*

≶GASP!≶ *W-WAIT! NO!* D-DON'T POINT YOUR *DISINTEGRATOR FINGER* AT ME!

"DISINTEG --?"

AAAGGGHH!

HUH?

WELL, WHAT DO YOU KNOW?

ALIEN!

PSYCHO!

WHO *SAYS* THERE'S NEVER A POLICE OFFICER AROUND WHEN YOU NEED ONE?

IT HELPS IF THERE'S A *CONCERNED CITIZEN* NEARBY WITH A *CELL PHONE.*

BREAK IT UP! YOU'RE BOTH *UNDER ARREST!*

ASSAULT AND BATTERY, DISTURBING THE PEACE...

NO, NO! YOU DON'T *UNDERSTAND!*

GO2

WE'RE BEING *INVADED!* HE'S AN *ALIEN!*

I AM *NOT!*

LOOKS LIKE *THEY* WON'T BE BOTHERING ANYONE FOR A WHILE.

WHY DO SOME PEOPLE GET SO *FREAKED OUT* BY ALIENS, ANYWAY?

Angela's

POLICE

I HAVE NO IDEA.

BUT WHEN THEY SAW YOUR *REAL FACE* --

-- *THEN* I COULD UNDERSTAND THEIR GETTING FREAKED OUT!

End

END OF AN ERA

Summer is almost out and it's time for Ben and Gwen to say goodbye to alien adventures for a while.

Ben is seriously grossed out that he has to hide the Omnitrix away and concentrate on his school studies – no more cosmic adventures, just rows of algebra and tons of rules.

SO NOT COOL!

BUT VILGAX WANTS TO STEAL THE OMNITRIX SO THERE'S TIME FOR ONE MORE SHOWDOWN! FOLLOW THE LINES TO FIND THE RIGHT PATH TO VILGAX SO BEN CAN KICK HIS BUTT ONCE AND FOR ALL!

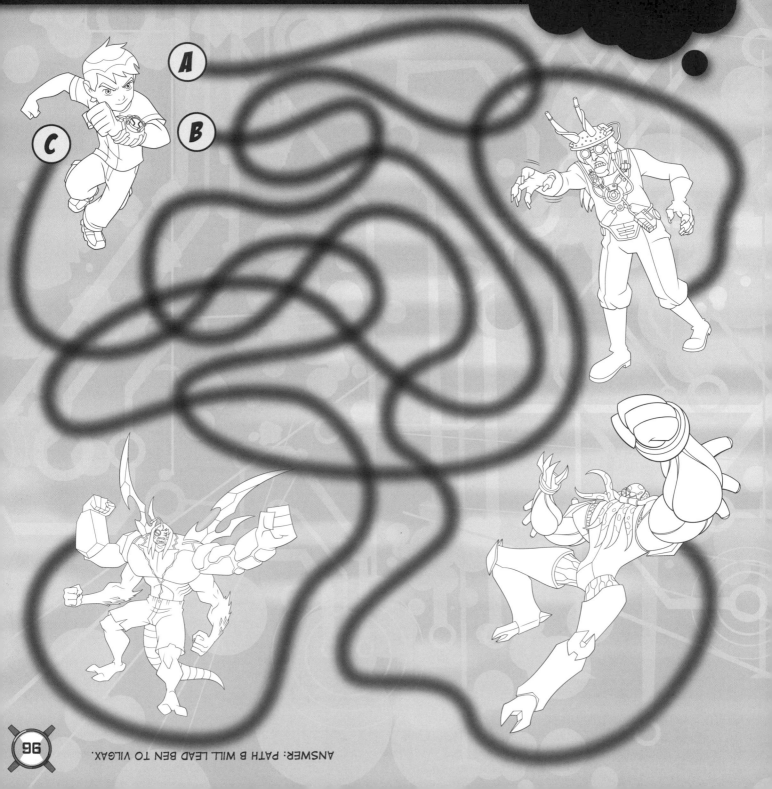

ANSWER: PATH B WILL LEAD BEN TO VILGAX.

OMNITRIX SECRETS

Now the Omnitrix needs to be locked away, safe from evil hands. It's your job to keep the code safe, so Vilgax can't intercept it. But first, you have to work out what it is.

1. TAKE THE LETTERS SHOWN FROM THE NAMES OF EACH OF THESE ALIENS ...

4TH LETTER, 7TH LETTER

GREY MATTER

6TH LETTER

DIAMONDHEAD

6TH LETTER, 10TH LETTER

GHOSTFREAK

2ND LETTER, 7TH LETTER

RIPJAWS

2. WRITE THEM DOWN HERE.

6TH LETTER

HEATBLAST

3. NOW UNJUMBLE THEM TO SPELL THE NAME OF ANOTHER ALIEN!

THIS IS YOUR SECRET CODE, SO KEEP IT SAFE AND SHOW IT TO NOBODY. SEE YOU ON THE OTHER SIDE ...!

WELCOME TO ALIEN FORCE!

FIVE YEARS
HAVE PASSED SINCE BEN LOCKED
THE OMNITRIX AWAY. BEN IS NOW
15-YEARS OLD. GRANDPA MAX HAS GONE
MISSING AND BEN HAS TO GO HERO ONCE
MORE! BUT THE OMNITRIX HAS CHANGED TOO -
NOW THERE ARE TEN NEW ALIEN HEROES TO GET
TO GRIPS WITH!

LUCKILY, BEN IS NOT ALONE. COUSIN GWEN IS
HERE TO HELP, AND SHE NOW HAS SOME PRETTY
AWESOME SUPERPOWERS OF HER OWN. SO HAS
KEVIN LEVIN, ALIAS KEVIN 11 - IF HE CAN JUST
LEAVE HIS BAD-BOY PAST BEHIND!

THERE ARE ALSO SOME EVIL NEW VILLAINS TO
FIGHT. THEY WANT TO TAKE OVER THE WORLD,
AND WILL STOP AT NOTHING ...

FEELING BRAVE?
THEN READ ON!

HOW IT BEGINS . . .

His name is Max Tennyson. We've had trouble with him before.

Then let this be the final time he troubles us.

Destroy him!

The story of Alien Force starts with the villains. A DNAlien tells the HighBreed Leader that someone has been leaking details of their secret operations to the authorities.

Then, Ben suddenly discovers that his Grandpa Max has gone missing. Add to that his very first encounter with a scary DNAlien and a warning message from Max and Ben knows it's time to go hero again!

Ben, Gwen and Kevin come up against three main groups of villains – the HighBreed, DNAliens and the Forever Knights – in addition to a few lesser-known bad guys. Looks like it's battle time!

MAX'S WARNING

Grandpa Max has left Ben an important message. But Ben is having trouble deciphering the code.

Can you work it out? Follow the circle in a clockwise direction starting at the top, and write every third letter in the space below.

_____ __ ___
___ _____
_____ _____.

THE OMNITRIX

It's time to bring the new Omnitrix to life! Find an Omnitrix sticker and place it in the holding cell opposite. Then carefully copy it into the big box. Go slow now ... you don't want the Omnitrix to malfunction!

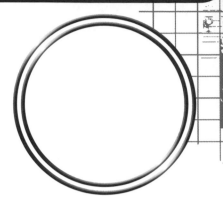

EVIL MESSAGE

The HighBreed are Ben's most powerful enemy. They are believed to be the first intelligent life forms ever! But what do they want with planet Earth?

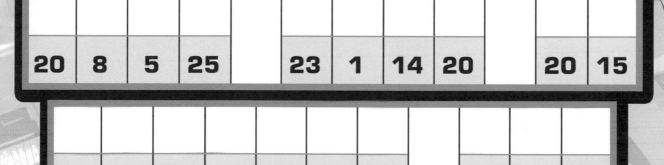

A	B	C	D	E	F	G	H	I	J	K	L	M
1	2	3	4	5	6	7	8	9	10	11	12	13

N	O	P	Q	R	S	T	U	V	W	X	Y	Z
14	15	16	17	18	19	20	21	22	23	24	25	26

20	8	5	25		23	1	14	20		20	15

3	12	5	1	14	19	5		20	8	5

21	14	9	22	5	18	19	5		15	6

1	12	12		18	1	3	5	19		2	21	20

20	8	5	13	19	5	12	22	5	19

KEViN E. LEViN

After dealing in illegal alien technology and spending time in the Null Void (an extra-dimensional prison), 16-year-old Kevin has now turned his back on crime and has joined forces with Ben and Gwen in the fight against evil.

"TAKE YOUR BEST SHOT"

STRENGTHS

• Kevin has the power to absorb any solid material, such as wood, metal, steel and concrete — making him capable of lending some serious muscle!

• He is very knowledgeable about the bad guys and their alien technology.

WEAKNESSES

• Although he is now mostly a reformed character, Kevin can still sometimes be tempted to steal goods and equipment from the villains.

• Kevin can be headstrong and stubborn.

KEVIN'S CAR

Kevin provides the wheels for the team and drives this cool green sports car from the 1970s. It's the ultimate action cruiser, filled with hidden alien technology and battle capabilities.

NUMBER RESCUE

The DNAliens are descending and Gwen's magical orbs are failing. Can you show Kevin the quickest path to Gwen before it's too late? The quickest path is the route with the smallest total when the numbers are added together.

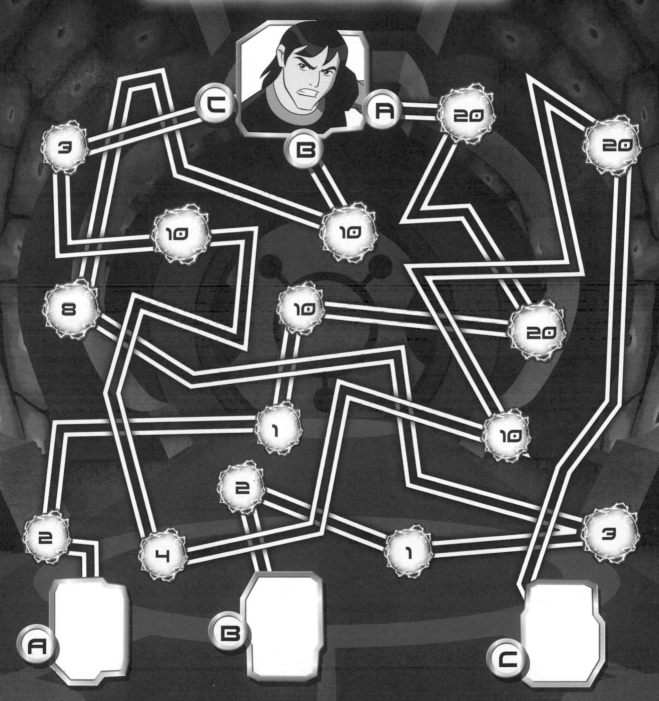

ECHO ECHO

Echo Echo might be small and compact, but he's big in power. A living amplifier, Echo Echo can scream at high-pitched ultrasonic frequencies – enough to shatter steel, overload machinery and stop missiles in mid-flight.

GOOD GUY

ECHO ECHO FACT FILE

HE HAS AN EAR-PIERCING, ULTRASONIC SCREAM.

ECHO ECHO CAN CHANNEL VIBRATIONS, AMPLIFY SOUNDS AND USE ECHOLOCATION.

HE CAN MAKE AS MANY COPIES OF HIMSELF AS HE LIKES – HANDY FOR CONFUSING THE BAD GUYS!

ECHO DUPLICATION

Echo Echo has duplicated his name horizontally in the grid below. How many times can you see his full name? Write your answer in the blank box.

E	C	H	P	E	C	H	O	E	C	H	O
E	H	C	O	E	C	H	O	E	H	C	O
E	C	H	O	E	C	H	O	E	O	H	O
E	H	C	O	E	C	H	O	E	H	C	O
E	C	H	O	E	C	H	O	E	C	H	E
C	H	O	E	C	H	O	E	C	H	O	E
C	H	E	C	H	O	E	C	H	O	E	E
O	H	E	C	H	O	E	H	C	O	E	C
O	O	E	C	H	E	C	H	O	O	E	H
C	O	E	C	H	O	E	C	H	O	E	H
C	O	E	C	H	O	E	C	H	E	C	O
E	E	C	H	O	E	C	H	O	E	C	H

NO WAY!

SOMEBODY *JACKED* MY *RIDE!* WE WERE ONLY GONE WHAT, A HALF HOUR?

GEEZ, KEVIN. ALL THOSE LEVEL 5 ALIEN GADGETS, AND YOU NEVER PUT IN A BURGLAR ALARM?

JULIE? GOTTA CANCEL OUT. YES, AGAIN...

I THOUGHT HERO TIME WAS OVER.

BUT EVER SINCE I PUT THE OMNITRIX BACK ON, IT'S LIKE THERE'S A NEW THREAT ALL THE TIME.

I GOT A *BUNCH* OF ALARMS, GWEN. TRACKING DEVICES, TOO. BUT NOTHING'S SHOWING UP.

ESPECIALLY SINCE I LOST GRANDPA MAX TO THE HIGHBREED. NOW IT'S ALL ON ME.

SO, THIS IS A THING.

GWEN? ANY CHANCE YOU CAN FIND THE CAR?

THE NEW ORDER

WRITER: MATT WAYNE / ARTIST: ROB HAYNES
LETTERER: RANDY GENTILE / CO-EDITORS: GEHRLEIN & HILTY
BEN 10 CREATED BY MAN OF ACTION

GOOP

Goop is a really cool alien, because basically he's a blob of green, runny, shape-shifting slime! He has a **UFO**-like device above his head which can cause Goop's slime to take any shape and even hover off the ground. Goop is a really slick mover, but he can be a bit messy!

GOOD GUY

GOOP FACT FILE

CAN MIMIC THE SHAPE OF SIMPLE OBJECTS TO FOOL OPPONENTS.

HE IS BEN'S MOST VERSATILE ALIEN FORM.

HE CAN EXPEL A HIGHLY CORROSIVE ACID AND USE THIS AS A WEAPON.

IDENTi-GOOP

Goop has the amazing power to turn into the shape of any simple object. What would you turn into, if you were Goop? Perhaps a phone, a boat or a carton of milkshake? Draw your design here.

HUMUNGOUSAUR

Humungousaur is Ben's largest and most powerful alien form. He's a huge dinosaur alien, and is able to increase his body size and weight whenever the job calls for it!

HUMUNGOUSAUR FACT FILE

HUMUNGOUSAUR'S THICK LAYER OF SKIN PROTECTS HIM FROM MOST ATTACKS.

HE CAN GROW TO AN AMAZING 18 METRES IN HEIGHT.

WHEN HE GROWS, HE DEVELOPS DINOSAUR-LIKE SPIKES ON HIS HEAD, BACK AND TAIL.

DRAW HUMUNGOUSAUR

Draw over the grey lines to create your own Humungousaur!

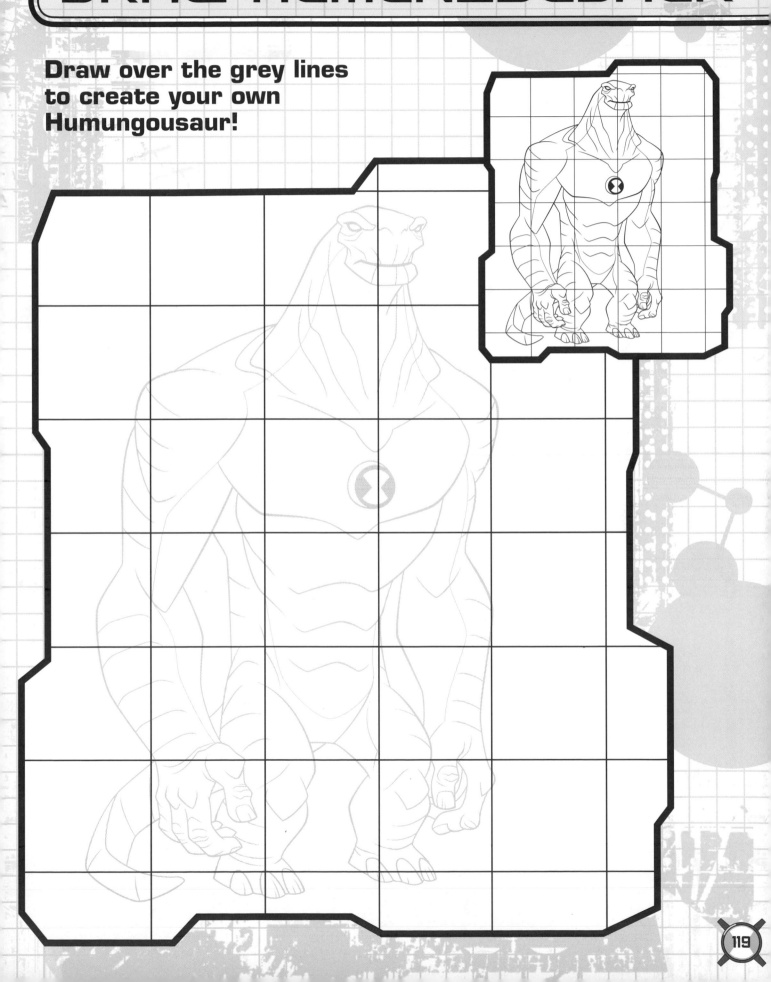

JET RAY

Whenever Ben needs speed, he turns into Jet Ray! Jet Ray is a manta-ray-like alien capable of flying and swimming faster than the speed of sound. He can attack an enemy by firing vicious neuroshock blasts from his eyes and tail.

GOOD GUY

JET RAY FACT FILE

HIS HOME PLANET (AEROPELA) IS COMPLETELY COVERED IN WATER – WHICH IS WHY HE HAS DEVELOPED TO EITHER FLY OR SWIM.

HE CAN MANOEUVRE EASILY AS HE FLIES AT TOP SPEEDS, HELPING HIM DODGE ATTACKS.

HE HAS WEBBED ARMS AND POISONOUS STINGERS ON HIS HEAD.

ZONE IN

Can you spot five things that are missing in picture 2? Quickly draw them back in so Jet Ray can blast some fire!

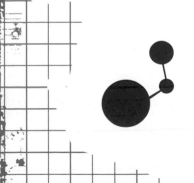

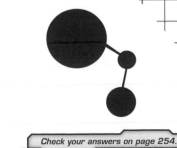

Check your answers on page 254.

SLIME ATTACK!

Read this awesome comic strip and draw pictures to match each scene. Use your stickers to help you!

A mutant slime is covering the skyscrapers of Washington DC!

Ben uses the Omnitrix to transform into Big Chill!

Gwen is trapped in the powerful slime!

Big Chill blows icy air at the slime. The slime freezes and Gwen is safe. For now . . .

WORD EXPLOSION

Make as many words as you can using the letters below. There are two done already to get you started.

ALIEN SUPERPOWERS

surprise

weapon

SWAMPFIRE

Swampfire is a plant-like alien and is Ben's first alien transformation in five years. He's like a living swamp who can produce highly flammable – and highly stinky – methane gas. Swampfire is extremely strong and has a regenerative ability that allows him to tunnel underground in vine form and root himself into the ground.

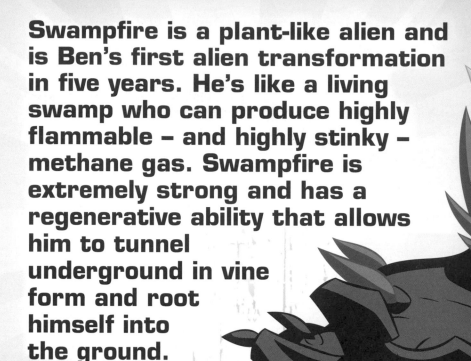

SWAMPFIRE FACT FILE

AS HE IS MADE OF MUD, HE IS JUST ABOUT SAFE FROM ALL PHYSICAL HARM, AS THINGS GO RIGHT THROUGH HIM!

HE CAN SHOOT FLAMES FROM HIS HANDS LIKE A FLAMETHROWER.

HE IS ABLE TO REGENERATE SEVERED LIMBS – HIS OWN, AND ANYONE ELSE'S.

TANGLED ROOTS

Swampfire has thrown out some vine roots to trap a nasty villain. Follow the trails to work out which one leads to the bad guy. Then, can you identify the baddy from his shadow? Write his name on the dotted line.

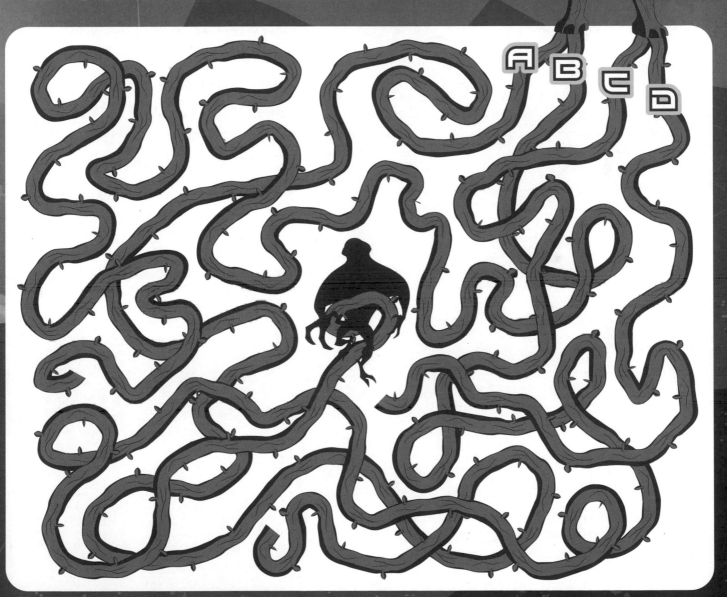

The bad guy is a _____

CHROMASTONE

ChromaStone is a real tough guy! He is a living crystal, his body made up of almost indestructible silicone. He can absorb energy (like a conductor) and channel it into laser blasts. ChromaStone has superhuman strength and there is almost nothing that can harm him.

GOOD GUY

CHROMASTONE FACT FILE

HAS SHARDS OF TOUGH CRYSTAL ATTACHED TO HIS HEAD, CHEST AND BACK.

LASER BEAMS BLASTED AT HIM BY ALIEN WEAPONS BOUNCE STRAIGHT OFF HIS BODY.

CAN ABSORB RADIATION AND TRANSFORM IT INTO ANY KIND OF LIGHT (INCLUDING LASERS).

CHROMASTONE CHECK OUT

One of these pictures of ChromaStone is a fake.
It will look different to the rest. Can you spot it?

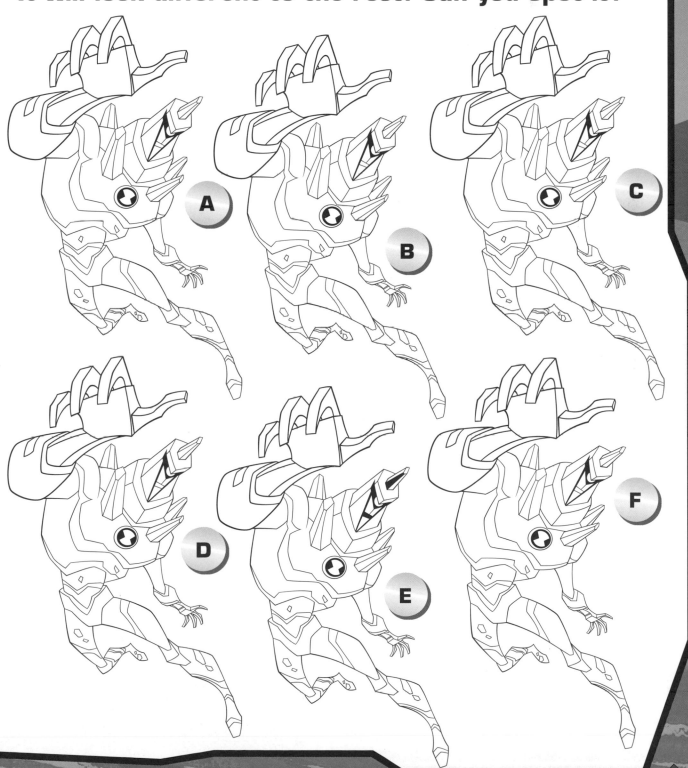

Answer: E is different. ChromaStone's mouth and spike are black.

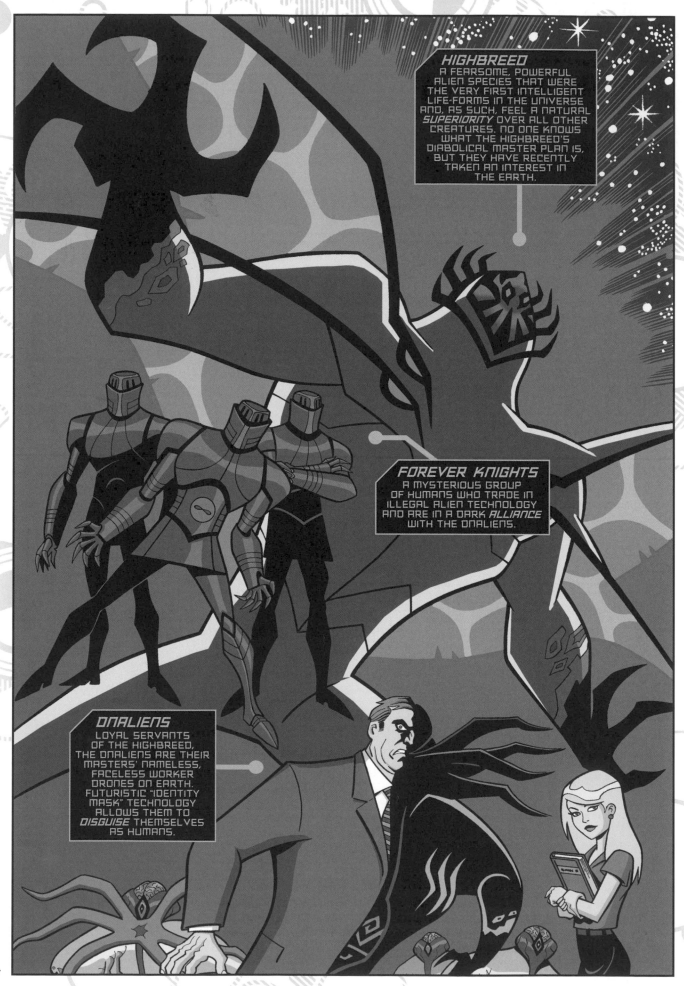

HIGHBREED
A FEARSOME, POWERFUL ALIEN SPECIES THAT WERE THE VERY FIRST INTELLIGENT LIFE-FORMS IN THE UNIVERSE AND, AS SUCH, FEEL A NATURAL *SUPERIORITY* OVER ALL OTHER CREATURES. NO ONE KNOWS WHAT THE HIGHBREED'S DIABOLICAL MASTER PLAN IS, BUT THEY HAVE RECENTLY TAKEN AN INTEREST IN THE EARTH.

FOREVER KNIGHTS
A MYSTERIOUS GROUP OF HUMANS WHO TRADE IN ILLEGAL ALIEN TECHNOLOGY AND ARE IN A DARK *ALLIANCE* WITH THE DNALIENS.

DNALIENS
LOYAL SERVANTS OF THE HIGHBREED, THE DNALIENS ARE THEIR MASTERS' NAMELESS, FACELESS WORKER DRONES ON EARTH. FUTURISTIC "IDENTITY MASK" TECHNOLOGY ALLOWS THEM TO *DISGUISE* THEMSELVES AS HUMANS.

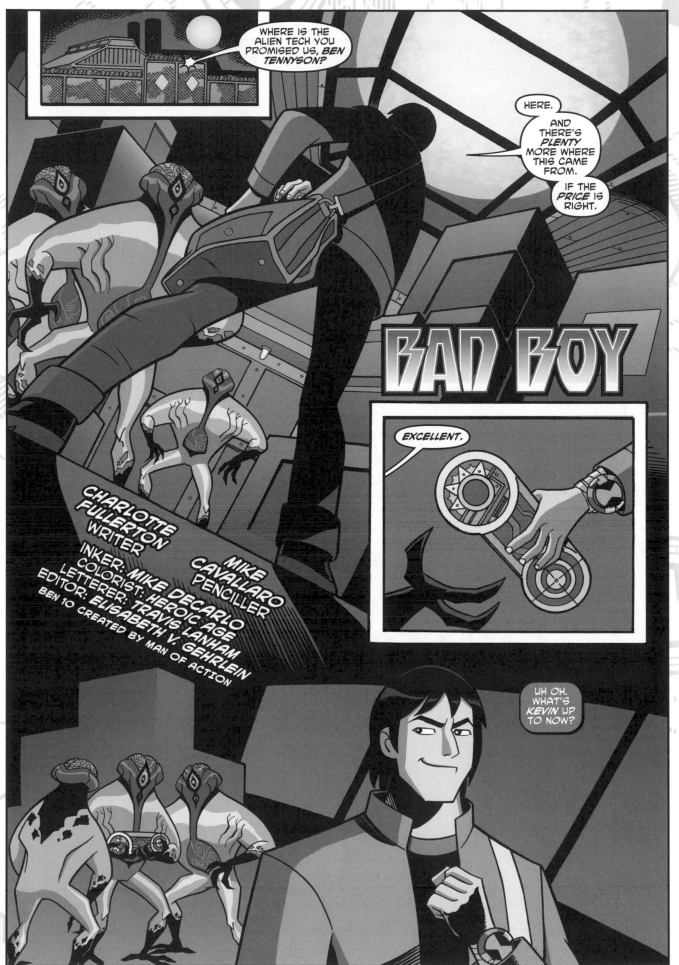

WHERE IS THE ALIEN TECH YOU PROMISED US, *BEN TENNYSON?*

HERE. AND THERE'S *PLENTY* MORE WHERE THIS CAME FROM.

IF THE *PRICE* IS RIGHT.

BAD BOY

EXCELLENT.

CHARLOTTE FULLERTON
WRITER

MIKE CAVALLARO
PENCILLER

INKER: MIKE DECARLO
COLORIST: HEROIC AGE
LETTERER: TRAVIS LANHAM
EDITOR: ELISABETH V. GEHRLEIN
BEN 10 CREATED BY MAN OF ACTION

UH OH. WHAT'S *KEVIN* UP TO NOW?

"YOU KNOW, BEN, I WASN'T SURE *HOW* YOU WERE GOING TO TAKE THE NEWS THAT KEVIN HAS TURNED OUT TO BE SO *UNTRUSTWORTHY.*"

"BUT I NEVER WOULD HAVE GUESSED YOU'D BE *HAPPY* ABOUT IT!"

"ARE YOU JUST TRYING TO RUB IT IN? THAT THE GUY I *LIKE* IS STILL ONE OF THE *BAD* GUYS AFTER ALL?

"'CAUSE THAT'S *REAL* MATURE OF YOU."

I KNOW EXACTLY WHAT KEVIN'S BEEN DOING, GWEN. BECAUSE *I'M* THE ONE WHO *PUT HIM UP TO IT!*

BEEP BEEP BEEP

;GASP;

THAT WAS A *SIGNAL* FROM KEVIN! SOMETHING'S GONE WRONG!

TIME FOR THE *REAL BEN TENNYSON* TO SWING INTO ACTION, AS--

SPIDERMONKEY!

WHY DIDN'T YOU AND KEVIN LET *ME* IN ON YOUR LITTLE *PLAN?* WHATEVER IT IS.

KEVIN MADE ME PROMISE NOT TO. IN CASE ANYTHING WENT *WRONG*, HE DIDN'T WANT YOU IN HARM'S WAY.

GREAT. AND LOOK WHO *DID* END UP IN *HARM'S WAY!*

UH, IT'S THE *THOUGHT* THAT COUNTS?

YOU HAVE DELIVERED THE *OMNITRIX* RIGHT INTO THE HANDS OF THE *HIGHBREED!* FOOLISH *BEN TENNYSON!*

THAT'S MY NAME. DON'T WEAR IT OUT.

I AM!

THAT'S *NOT* BEN TENNYSON!

HEY. HOW YA DOING?

BETTER NOW.

DESTROY THEM *BOTH*.

AAAND I'M BACK TO DOING NOT SO GOOD.

GRAHRGH!

EW. THAT'S *DISGUSTING!*

SPLOOP

LIKE *THAT'S* NOT?

CLANG

STOP! OR I'LL DESTROY WHAT YOU'RE BOTH *REALLY* HERE FOR...

...THIS *ALIEN TECH* BELONGING TO ONE *MAXWELL TENNYSON!*

SLURRR

GRANDPA MAX!

HOW DOES THE HIGHBREED KNOW WHAT OUR PLAN'S *REALLY* BEEN ABOUT ALL THIS TIME, KEVIN?

LUCKY *GUESS*, I GUESS.

OUR DNALIENS MAY BE MINDLESS DRONES, BUT YOU *CANNOT OUTSMART* THE HIGHBREED!

WE ARE *SUPERIOR* TO ALL CREATURES IN EVERY WAY!

IN *EVERY* WAY?

CHOOM

GWEN!

ONE OF YOU GET THE *TECH!*

KEVIN?

COSMIC SEARCH

Can you find these evil words in the grid below?
Words can read up, down, across and diagonally.

Forever Knights	Evil	Weapons
Ammunition	Galaxy	Destroy
HighBreed	Villains	Armour
DNAliens	Zombies	Battle

```
Y X H I G H B R E E D S Y T F
O S Z B A C F W V S N D S D O
R T Y N L B Y B I W A C X Z R
T Y K X A Q F M L C L K H B E
S C V W X Z S X Q Z I N D K V
E W G R Y F B U J Z E C Y B E
D S E Q W K V D A P N C Z J R
W X T A B P J R T K S F B S K
F C Q V P A M M U N I T I O N
Z X D W Q O T S D K B V X K I
R F S K U L N T V S Y W Z D G
Y M P R F C R S L B X D C L H
X T K B D Y K S F E L G T J T
Z O M B I E S V I L L A I N S
```

DESIGN ALIEN TECH

Alien technology is getting more and more advanced. Can you design your own awesome piece of alien ammunition to help Ben kick some serious butt?

AMMUNITION NAME: _____

WHAT IT DOES: _____

_____

BiG CHiLL

As a flying ghost, Big Chill is pretty creepy! He looks a bit like a blue moth, and when he folds up his wings and antennae, he has a spooky hooded appearance. He is incredibly strong but his main weapon is his chilly breath that can freeze anything solid.

GOOD GUY

BIG CHILL FACT FILE

HE'S A GHOST WHO CAN PASS THROUGH ANYTHING.

BIG CHILL CAN MAKE HIMSELF INVISIBLE.

HE CAN DROP THE TEMPERATURE OF ANYTHING TO FREEZING POINT.

FREEZE OVER

Where do you think Big Chill comes from? Imagine a freezing planet and draw it in the frame below. You could add snow, mountains, frozen lakes and anything else you can think of. Add icicle stickers, too!

SPIDERMONKEY

His name says it all! A cross between a spider and a monkey, Spidermonkey is Ben's most agile alien. He can spin awesome giant spiderwebs and stick to walls – skills that prove really useful when trapping the bad guys.

GOOD GUY

SPIDERMONKEY FACT FILE

A NIMBLE MONKEY-LIKE ALIEN, WITH SIX LIMBS.

HIS SPIDERWEBS ARE MADE OF SILK AS HARD AS STEEL CABLE.

A CHATTERING, MISCHIEVOUS ALIEN WHO SOMETIMES SCREECHES LIKE A MONKEY.

LET'S MONKEY AROUND!

Use your pencil powers to draw in Spidermonkey's four arms and two legs. Awesome!

RESCUE MISSION

The DNAliens have captured Gwen! They've sprayed poisonous gases into the air so Kevin can't find his way. Can you show him the path to Gwen before it's too late?

Beware! Choose the wrong path and Kevin could collide with one of the evil villains.

Check your answer on page 255.

OMNITRIX MIX-UP

The Omnitrix is malfunctioning. Unscramble the names below so Ben can kick some serious alien butt!

When you've worked them out, find the alien stickers so the Omnitrix is ready for action.

1

Y A J
R T E

_ _ _ _ _ _

2

B C I L
G I H L

_ _ _ _ _ _ _

3

T B M O I
N A R R S

_ _ _ _ _ _ _ _ _ _

4

A
M W P R E S F I

_ _ _ _ _ _ _ _ _

BRAIN STORM

With his crab-like body, Brain Storm looks like a seafood platter! But appearances can be deceptive, and Brain Storm is a genius – Ben's most intelligent alien. He is also physically powerful, with sharp pincers and a tough exoskeleton.

BRAIN STORM FACT FILE

CAN OPEN HIS SHELL TO REVEAL HIS HUGE BRAIN.

HE CAN CONTROL ELECTRICAL ENERGY JUST BY THINKING HARD ENOUGH.

WITH ENOUGH CONCENTRATION, BRAIN STORM CAN EVEN LEVITATE IN THE AIR!

GOOD GUY

TAKE IT SLOW

Copy Brain Storm into the grid, square by square.

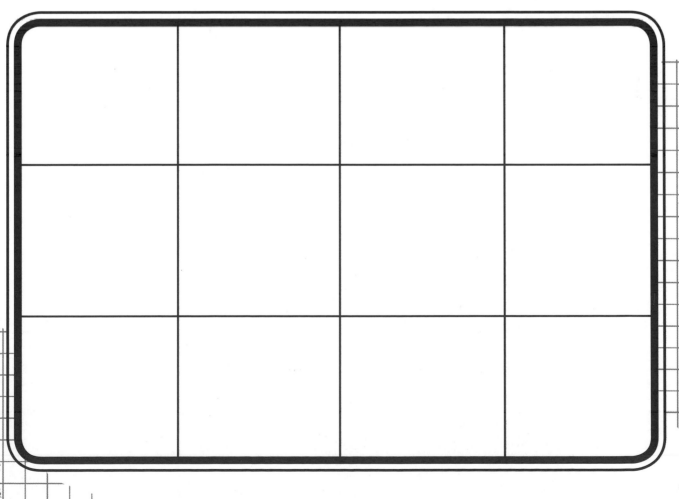

ALIEN X

Alien X is Ben's most powerful form and also the most mysterious and dangerous. Alien X has three distinct personalities – Serena (the voice of love), Bellicus (the voice of rage) and Ben (the voice of reason).

GOOD GUY

ALIEN X FACT FILE

TWO OF ALIEN X'S PERSONALITIES MUST BE IN AGREEMENT FOR HIM TO BE ABLE TO DO ANYTHING.

HE CAN WARP REALITY.

ALIEN X IS BEN'S LEAST FAVOURITE ALIEN FORM.

X-POWER

Find an Omnitrix sticker to add to Alien X's chest. Why not draw a mysterious planet in the background?

That a boy, Ship, roll over. Now sit up and beg.

Ship! Ship!

Having a little *alien* for a *pet* is the best!

Hey, *Julie!*

Hi, *Ben.* I've been teaching Ship some *new tricks.* Want to see?

Maybe later. I've got a *surprise* for you.

A *present?* For me? You *shouldn't have.* But I'm awfully *glad* you did. Heh.

It's a *friendship necklace.* I made it myself.

Oh, Ben. How *thoughtful!*

SHIP SHAPE

WRITER • CHARLOTTE FULLERTON   ART & COVER • MIN S. KU
LETTERER • TRAVIS LANHAM   COLORIST • HEROIC AGE
EDITORS • ELISABETH V. GEHRLEIN & SEAN RYAN
BEN 10 CREATED BY MAN OF ACTION

It's so *beautiful!* I've never seen a *stone* like this before.

I found it on my last adventure in outer *space.* A *special gem* for a *special girl.*

MORPHH

SHIP!

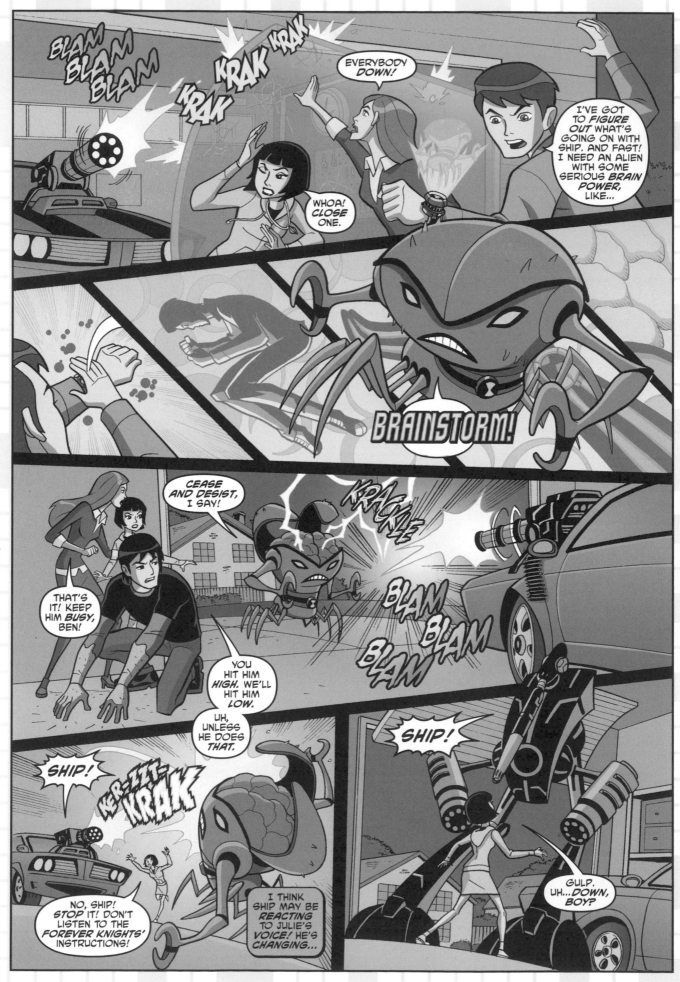

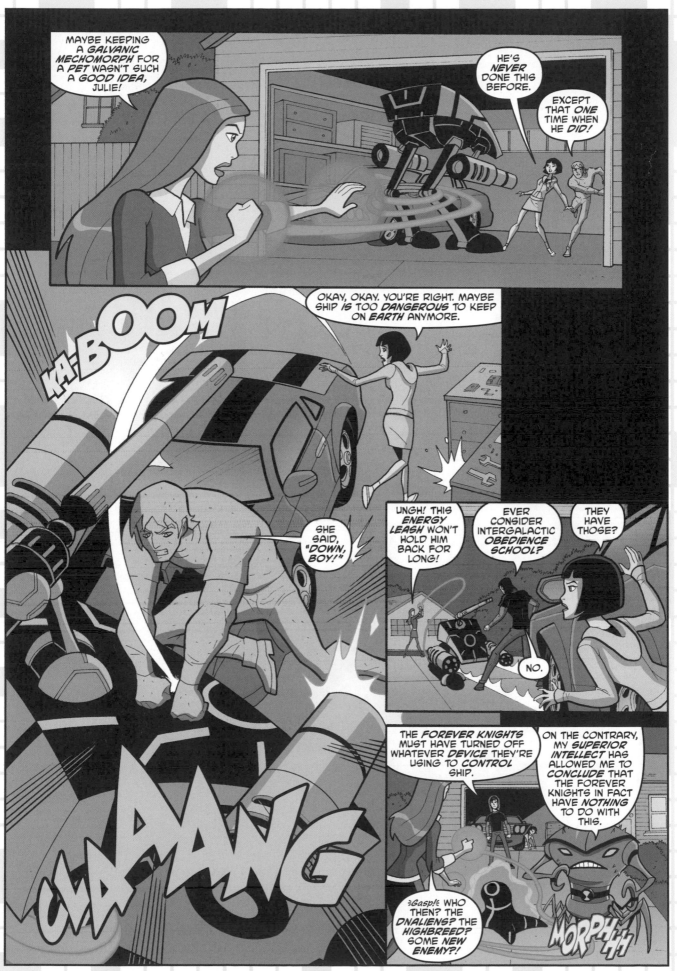

TAKE THE TEST

The time has come to test your alien knowledge.
How well do you know the secrets of the force?
Pass the test and you're in the game!
Fail and you still have a lot to learn.

1 Who owns a car?

a) Gwen
b) Ben
c) Kevin

2 Which alien can turn invisible?

a) Swampfire
b) Big Chill
c) Echo Echo

3 Who are the loyal servants to the HighBreed?

a) DNAliens
b) The Forever Knights
c) Alien X and ChromaStone

4 What is Kevin's superpower?

a) he can absorb metal, wood and stone
b) he can fly
c) he can morph into a dragon

5 **Which alien has six limbs?**

a) Goop
b) Spidermonkey
c) Swampfire

6 **How many years did Ben leave the Omnitrix for?**

a) 7
b) 2
c) 5

7 **What is the name of the intergalactic police force that Grandpa Max is a member of?**

a) HighBreed
b) Plumbers
c) Drillers

8 **Which alien is so powerful his mere thoughts become reality?**

a) Alien X
b) Brain Storm
c) Spidermonkey

Answers: 1 – c, 2 – b, 3 – a, 4 – a, 5 – b, 6 – c, 7 – b, 8 – a.

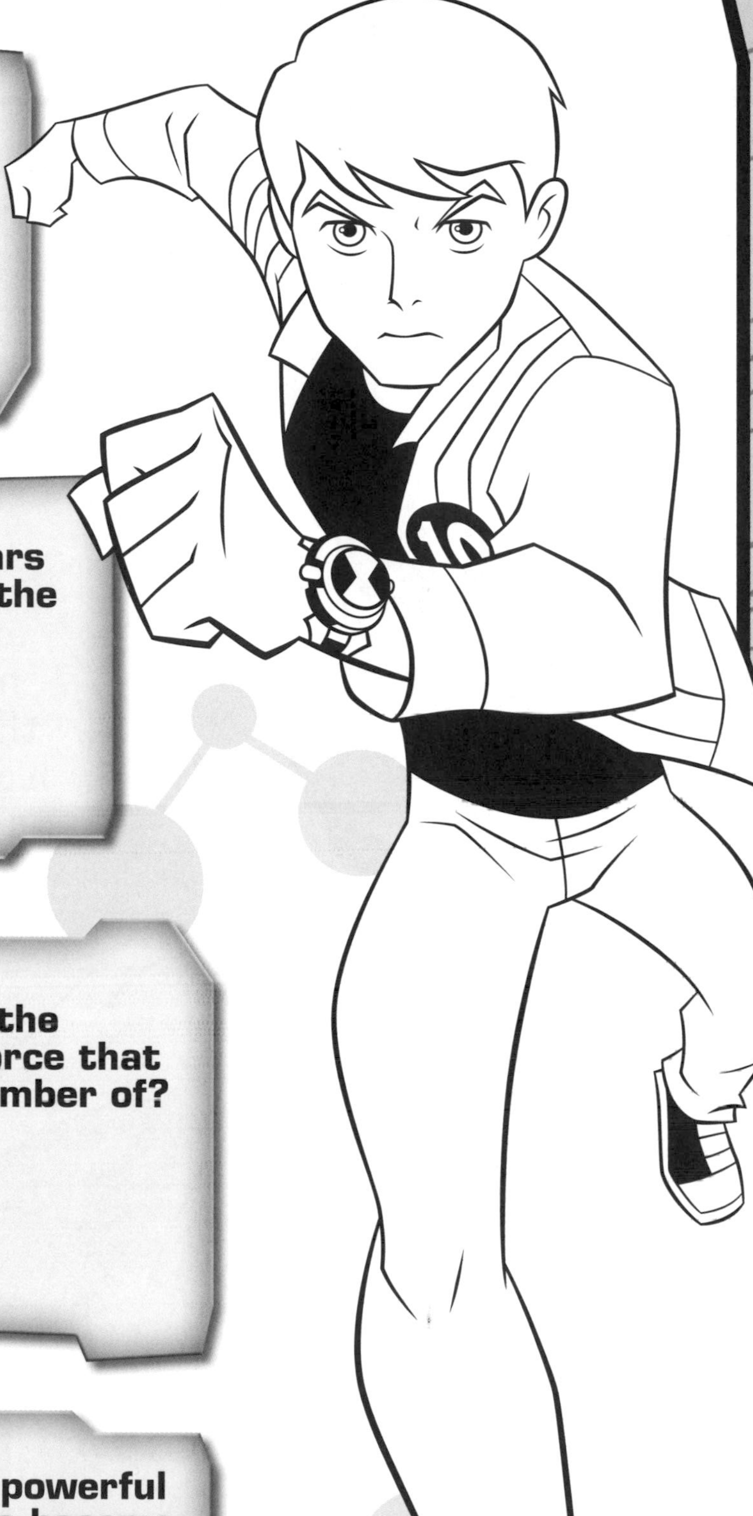

Ben, Gwen, Kevin and Grandpa Max come up against three main groups of villains in Alien Force – the HighBreed, DNAliens and the Forever Knights.

THE HIGHBREED

The HighBreed are power crazy. They are an alien race from the planet Darama, and they are Ben and the gang's most dangerous enemy. They think of themselves as the highest life-form in the universe and believe that they were the very first race ever to exist.

HIGHBREED ID

- Tall, humanoid beings with fold-out wings on their back.

- Hugely powerful — can overpower aliens larger than themselves.

- Can fire their fingertips like darts.

The HighBreed are determined to cleanse the universe of all races except themselves – and Earth is their next target! They think that coming into contact with other races will contaminate them, and they have DNAliens to do their dirty work for them.

DNALIENS

DNAliens are hybrids of humans and aliens, and they are servants of the HighBreed. They are sneaky, and are able to disguise themselves as humans using special identity masks.

DNAliens are created by attaching a facehugger-like parasite called a Xenocyte to a human host.

DNALIEN ID

- Pale brown skin with vicious tentacles in their chest.

- Fairly strong and are able to spit out a horrible sticky slime.

- They prefer cold climates and build weather control centres.

FOREVER KNIGHTS

The Forever Knights are a secret society first formed during the Middle Ages – with the purpose of slaying a dragon. They now trade in illegal alien technology, using it for their own personal power.

FOREVER KNIGHTS ID

- Like true knights, they wear a complete suit of body armour.

- They use powerful laser lances as weapons.

- They trade with the HighBreed, and use DNAliens as go-betweens.

BATTLE TIME!

An evil villain is coming to attack you! Copy the creepy details to fill in his body. Then blast him with fireball stickers!

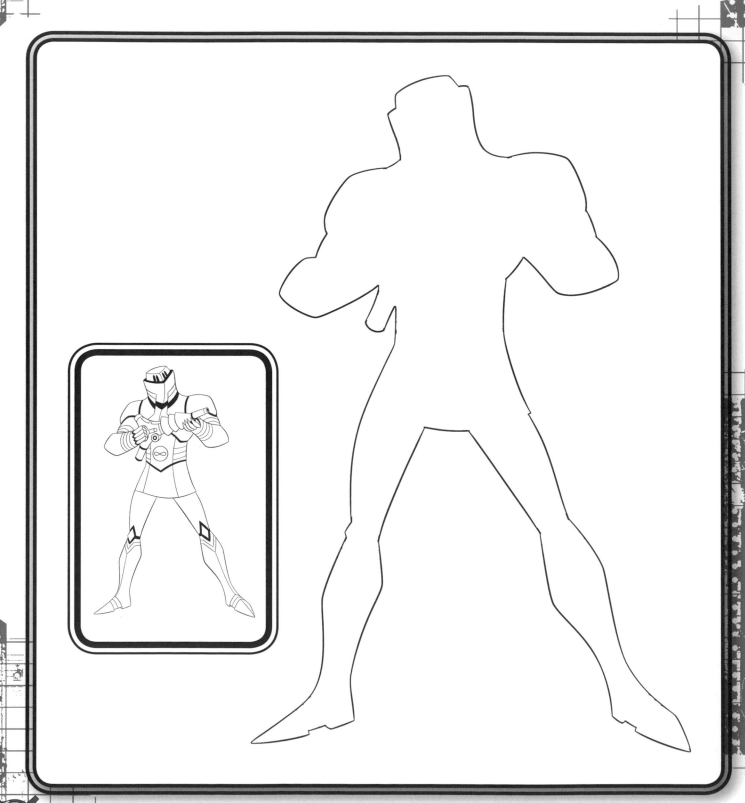

VILLAIN ALERT

The HighBreed, DNAliens and the Forever Knights are a massive threat to planet Earth. Think up a new evil villain and draw it in the space below.

NAME: _____

SUPERPOWER: _____

EVIL THREAT: _____

SQUARE OFF

The battle is on! You will need someone to challenge in this battle of concentration. Take turns drawing a straight line between any two black dots. If the line you draw completes a square, put your initials in it and take another shot. When all the dots have been connected, the player with most points wins!

SCORES: Player 1: _____ points. Player 2: _____ points.

CHROMA-SEARCH

When you've conquered this wordsearch, look at the **10th** row and write down all the unused letters. Then unscramble them to reveal something that **ChromaStone** uses in battle!

Swampfire	ChromaStone	Brain Storm	Jet Ray
Big Chill	Ben	Max	Alien X
Goop	Kevin	Gwen	

S	A	B	I	G	C	H	I	L	L	R	S
A	W	M	T	E	N	R	O	P	T	B	T
L	P	A	E	C	H	V	G	O	O	P	E
I	L	X	M	N	S	B	N	U	B	E	M
N	M	W	N	P	R	H	E	O	S	L	O
M	C	A	B	B	F	A	N	L	R	R	L
B	H	S	L	L	R	I	S	A	P	E	P
X	R	T	O	I	A	L	R	J	I	U	J
B	O	A	P	L	E	X	R	E	G	S	B
L	M	A	I	S	E	N	R	T	W	S	E
F	A	L	E	N	E	S	X	R	E	W	N
G	S	D	R	V	S	L	I	A	N	Q	I
W	T	F	R	B	R	T	N	Y	R	R	E
D	O	S	F	N	J	B	O	S	T	N	N
T	N	E	K	E	V	I	N	R	N	E	X
M	E	R	S	A	N	P	O	V	M	P	P

Collected letters:

ChromaStone uses _____ to fight with!

HOW TO DRAW THE DNALIENS

The **DNAliens** use 'Identity Mask' technology, which allows them to disguise themselves as other beings. They're not in disguise today though. It's your job to bring them to life!

1 Draw the frame lines. Add in lines for the arms and legs. Sketch a circle for the head.

2 Sketch the body. The legs are thin and narrow, the upper body is wide and heavy.

3 Draw wiggly lines to show the jelly-like brain. Gross! Add markings to the stomach, too.

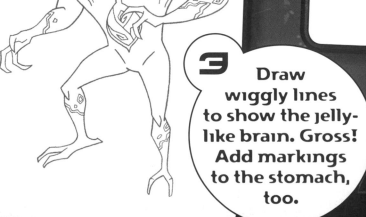

Practise drawing your DNAlien here!

METAL MERGE

Kevin has the amazing power to absorb solid materials just by touching them – such as metal, wood or stone. Try to imagine what he'd look like if he touched a brick wall, or a wooden bridge. Draw your design here!

MOONLIGHT SHADOWS

Which shadow belongs to which alien? The shadows are in different poses to confuse you!

Answers: 1 – B, 2 – A, 3 – E, 4 – D, 5 – C.

HOW TO DRAW GOOP

Goop is a green blob that can morph into any shape, from oozing slime balls to bouncy goo, there's no end to his shape-shifting powers!

1 Draw the frame lines. Sketch the outlines of his head and arms, too.

2 Draw a flowing line around your frame lines. Straight lines are too stiff for our gloopy friend.

3 Draw his slimy fingers. Do your usual clean-up, then grab a few shades of green to bring Goop to life!

HERO HiNT! When you have drawn Goop, why not draw him again in a different shape? Let's shape-shift!

Practise drawing Goop here! Add some goopy stickers when you have finished!

THE PAST IS THE KEY TO THE FUTURE

WRITER • *JASON HALL*   ARTIST • *MIN S. KU*
LETTERER • *TRAVIS LANHAM*   COLORIST • *HEROIC AGE*   EDITOR • *SEAN RYAN*
BEN 10: ALIEN FORCE CREATED BY *MAN OF ACTION*

THAT'S NOT GOOD...

BRILLIANT! YOU *ACTIVATED* THE THING AND KNOCKED THE ONLY ONE WITH THE ANSWERS *UNCONSCIOUS!*

I DIDN'T SEE *YOU* STEPPING UP WITH A MASTER PLAN!

59... 58... 57...

EASY, BOYS. THE RISING TESTOSTERONE LEVELS CAN'T BE HELPING--AND, BESIDES, I'VE GOT AN IDEA...

LET ME SEE IF I CAN *TRANSLATE* THESE--OH-BOY...WELL, IT'S A *BOMB.*

OH, *WONDERFUL...* NICE OF THEM TO MAKE IT COUNT DOWN IN *ENGLISH...*

IT WAS PLANTED HERE MANY YEARS AGO BY *THE HIGHBREED* WHEN THEY FIRST DEVISED THEIR PLAN TO "CLEANSE" THE EARTH OF ITS "FILTHY RACES". OH, NICE...

IT'S SORT OF A *DOOMSDAY/FINAL-SOLUTION* DEVICE MEANT TO *DESTROY THE PLANET* IF THINGS DON'T GO THEIR WAY.

OKAY, HERE'S THE DEAL. IT'S *HIGHLY ILLEGAL*, SO I'VE NEVER MENTIONED IT BEFORE.

I *KNOW* HOW YOU FEEL ABOUT MY...*COLORFUL PAST*.

IT'S A PIECE OF *"LEVEL 10" TECH* THAT SHOULDN'T EVEN BE IN THIS *ARM OF THE GALAXY*, LET ALONE *EARTH*.

IT'S A *"TEMPORAL BOOMERANG"* THAT'LL ALLOW US TO TAKE ONE FIVE-MINUTE ROUND TRIP... *BACK IN TIME*.

PERFECT! WE CAN JUST GO BACK A COUPLE MINUTES AND STOP OURSELVES FROM ARMING THE THING!

DO I HAVE TO EXPLAIN *TIME PARADOXES* TO YOU? WE NEED TO GO BACK TO WHEN YOU KNOW WHO HAD THE KEY AND GET IT.

LOOK, JUST *PICK A TIME*--THINK OF *WHEN* YOU WANT TO *GO*--

--AND I PRESS THIS BUTTON, AND WE'RE GONE..."

6...
5...
4...

AND SINCE I DON'T *REMEMBER* HAVING EVER *MET* MY *15-YEAR-OLD SELF* FROM THE FUTURE--

--I BETTER DISGUISE MYSELF JUST TO BE SAFE. *BIG CHILL!*

NOW YOU'RE GETTING THE IDEA. BUT WE *STILL* NEED TO MAKE SURE WE DON'T RUN INTO *OUR* YOUNGER SELVES.

NO SWEAT.

YEAH, RIGHT...

I WAS *CUTE*, HUH...?

HEH. WELL...

I'LL SHOW YOU SKILLS. MAYBE THERE'S SOMETHING IN HERE TO MAKE YOU SMELL BETTER...

THERE SHE GOES, WITH HER UGLY FACE BACK IN A BOOK. ANY WAY I CAN CONVINCE YOU TO KEEP IT THERE?

GOOD ONE, BEN...

NOW *WHERE* DID I KEEP MY *SUMO SLAMMER CARDS*...?

IT'S HERE!

HEY! DROP THE SUMO SLAMMER CARDS, PAL!

IT'S HERO TIME!

FWOOOOM

THAT REALLY *BURNS* ME UP! DO YOU KNOW *HOW LONG* IT TOOK ME TO BUILD THAT COLLECTION?

I ALWAYS *DID* HAVE A TEMPER.

TIME TO COOL OFF!

SHOOSH

BEN...?

WEIRD... I actually *REMEMBER* having this fight with some *CREEPY BLUE ALIEN* that I thought was after my *CARD COLLECTION!*

I always *THOUGHT* my *BIG CHILL* form seemed *VAGUELY FAMILIAR*--now I know *WHY!*

WHERE'D that creepy guy go?

WHO? *YOU'RE* the only creepy guy I see...

GOT IT!

WELL, *GOOD*-- since our *FIVE MINUTES* are up!

LET'S *BLOW* this time period...

BIP BIP BIP

BEN, HURRY!

I HOPE THIS--

4... 3... 2...

--WORKS!

1...DEVICE DISARMED.

TOO CLOSE, MAN!

WHEW! WELL, *THAT* was an *EXPERIENCE!* AND DEFINITELY *WEIRD* seeing ourselves back then.

WE SURE HAVE done a lot of *GROWING UP,* BEN.

YOU, GWEN? DEFINITELY. *BEN...?* THE JURY'S STILL OUT.

THANKS...

THE END

SNEAK INTO THE FUTURE

If you could go into the future, what do you think it would look like? What would the buildings look like? What vehicles would people use to get around?

The year is 2099. Draw a picture to bring it to life!

COMMUNICATOR

Ben has found a holoviewer containing a message from Grandpa Max. But the message is in code! Use the code breaker below to find out what Grandpa Max is saying.

9

8	1	22	5

20	8	5

15	13	14	9	20	18	9	24

SUPERHEROES

Read the following problems. Which of Ben's aliens would be best to cope with each situation? Write down the alien names, and add stickers of the aliens, too!

1 Ben needs to go in disguise. Who is his top shape-shifting alien?

1

2 Some plants are taking over the world. Who could control them?

2

3

3 The Forever Knights are firing lasers. Which alien could absorb the blasts?

4 The DNAliens are on the attack! Who can multiply themselves to kick some butt?

4

DESIGN ALIEN TECH

Everybody wants to get their hands on awesome alien technology! Can you design something to tip the intergalactic balance of power in Ben's favour?

TECH NAME:

....

WHAT IT DOES:

....

....

....

....

....

WHiCH ALiEN?

Read the clues below and check out the shadows.
Draw a line to match each alien shadow to that
alien's superpowers.

1 This nimble dude can stick to any wall.

A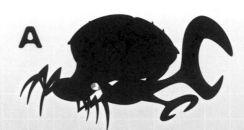

2 He can grow spikes on his back and tail.

B

3 He can create laser blasts.

C

4 This guy can produce fiery electrical storms.

D

Answers: 1-D (Spidermonkey), 2-C (Humungousaur), 3-B (ChromaStone), 4-A (Brain Storm).

MULTIPLICITY

How many times does Echo Echo appear in the box below?

GO BEN, GO!

Ben is an awesome superhero. Draw over the outline below, then colour him in!

CYBER GRID

Study this grid. The car, the Omnitrix, Alien X and Goop should appear once in each column, row and mini grid. Draw or write the names of the aliens and objects in the blank squares.

Check your answers on page 255.

HOW TO DRAW ECHO ECHO

Echo Echo is a walking amplifier. The sounds he makes are so loud he can shatter steel! Echo Echo might be small, but he can duplicate himself a limitless number of times. You could draw a whole army of Echo Echos!

1 Draw the frame lines, then sketch the shapes.

2 Carefully add the body and smaller details. Don't forget his Omnitrix symbol!

3 Now draw his secret backpack — he'll need this in battle!

Colouring should be easy — just green and black!

Practise drawing Echo Echo here!

ALIEN FRIENDS

Each of Ben's aliens has its own special characteristics. Check out the following alien notes, then try to match them up with people you know!

ECHO ECHO
Small with loud scream

HUMUNGOUSAUR
Big and strong

JET RAY
Fast swimmer

BRAIN STORM
Very clever

SPIDERMONKEY
Agile and acrobatic

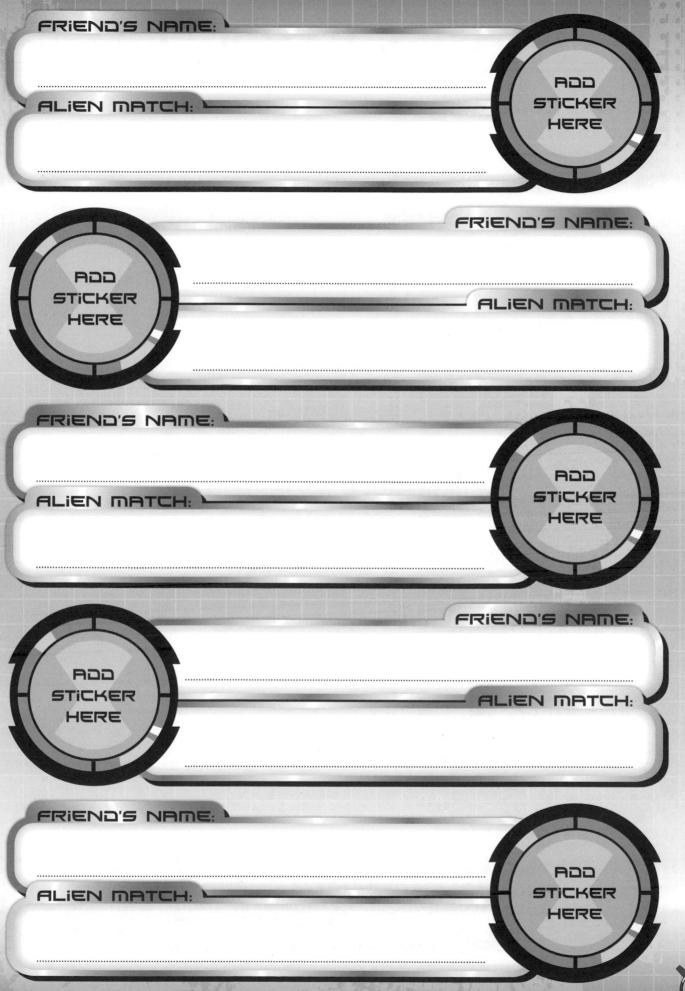

FRIEND'S NAME:

ALIEN MATCH:

ADD STICKER HERE

FRIEND'S NAME:

ADD STICKER HERE

ALIEN MATCH:

FRIEND'S NAME:

ALIEN MATCH:

ADD STICKER HERE

FRIEND'S NAME:

ADD STICKER HERE

ALIEN MATCH:

FRIEND'S NAME:

ALIEN MATCH:

ADD STICKER HERE

THE FINAL BATTLE

Before you can go any further, you must help Ben win the final battle! Evil Albedo has stolen his Omnitrix, but there's a new, more powerful watch-device waiting for Ben – the Ultimatrix! He just has to get past evil Vilgax and the DNAliens to reach it.

Can you guide Ben through the maze to the Ultimatrix to keep the adventures going? Don't crash into Vilgax or the DNAliens or you could lose everything!

**Did you make it through the maze alive?
Let's turn the page for some awesome
Ultimate Alien adventures ...**

WELCOME TO ULTIMATE ALIEN!

BEN 10 ULTIMATE ALIEN

AGE 16

ULTIMATE BEN 10

There's a time to go alien, and there's a time to go

ULTIMATE ...

Ben 10 is back, but this time his secret is out and he's a world-famous superstar! He's also got more alien forms with more incredible powers than ever before!

The Omnitrix has now been destroyed and in its place is the awesome **Ultimatrix** – a device that allows **Ben** to turn into brand new aliens as well as transforming into 'ultimate' versions of existing alien dudes.

With evil villains still threatening Earth and a global fanbase, it's a good job that Ben still has **Gwen** and **Kevin** by his side ...

LET'S GO ULTIMATE!

BEN TENNYSON

Ben is now 16 years old, and trying not to let international fame go to his head! It's lucky his girlfriend, Julie, helps keep his feet on the ground.

BEN FACTS

⌗ Ben now drives and has his own set of wheels – a cool green and black car.

⌗ He's still at high-school and has to juggle his alien life with everyday studying.

⌗ He now has a whole heap of brand new alien forms to master.

THE ULTIMATRIX

The Ultimatrix is an upgraded form of the Omnitrix. It not only gives Ben access to all of his original powers and abilities, but also lets him evolve his alien forms into even stronger and more powerful ultimate versions! The watch can also scan and store the DNA of any alien that is not already stored within it.

GWEN TENNYSON

Gwen is Ben's 16 year-old cousin. She has some amazing powers of her own, and they come in really handy when helping Ben fight the bad guys.

GWEN FACTS

- Gwen's grandma is an Anodite – an alien.
- Brave and full of energy, Gwen is also the brains of the gang.
- She can control magical beams, platforms and orbs.

ANODITE

Gwen was amazed to discover that her grandma is an Anodite – an alien. She had the chance to join her on the planet of Anodyne and learn how to master life energy, but she opted to stay on Earth with her friends and family and continue helping Ben.

KEVIN LEVIN

The son of a former Plumber (an intergalactic policeman), 17 year-old Kevin is tough and loves to get stuck in. He's mastered his own absorbing powers and is also Gwen's boyfriend.

KEVIN FACTS

- He used to be one of the bad guys, so he knows how they tick.
- Kevin knows about illegal alien technology, as he used to trade in it.
- He can absorb any solid material, like stone, wood or steel.

RUSTBUCKET III

The Rustbucket III is a very cool plane and spaceship. It belongs to Grandpa Max and it was a standard Plumber-issue ship, before Kevin made some improvements to it. After his car, the Rustbucket III is Kevin's pride and joy!

GRANDPA MAX

Max Tennyson is Ben and Gwen's Grandpa. He's a retired member of the Plumbers (the intergalactic police force) and is tough, brave and loyal. Max is always on hand to provide advice for the gang.

"At first I thought the attacks were random. I was wrong. They're organised."

JULIE YAMAMOTO

Julie is Ben's girlfriend. She thinks it's really cool that Ben can turn into aliens, and is pretty patient with him when he disappears to fight the bad guys. Julie's really bright, and she's also a talented tennis player.

FASHION VICTIM

WRITER: AMY WOLFRAM
ARTIST: ETHEN BEAVERS

COLORIST: HEROIC AGE
LETTERER: TRAVIS LANHAM
EDITOR: SEAN RYAN

BEN 10 ULTIMATE ALIEN
CREATED BY MAN OF ACTION

THEY'RE EVERYWHERE.

WHAT CAN I SAY? I'M A FASHION "DO."

YOU'LL NEVER CATCH ME IN ONE OF THOSE.

SALE!

EL COBRA

HEY! LET ME GO!

A MOB OF MY ADORING FANS MUST HAVE MISTAKEN HIM FOR ME.

MORE LIKE CHARMCASTER'S NON-ADORING ROCK MONSTERS!

COME FORTH, MY CREATURES. SEEK AND FIND. BEN TENNYSON WILL SOON BE MINE!

HA HA HA HA!!!

CHARMCASTER'S ROCK MONSTERS ARE ATTACKING ANYONE WEARING YOUR JACKET.

WHOA.

GUESS THAT MAKES YOU A FASHION "DON'T."

OH, NO. I'M NOT WEARING THAT!

IF YOU WANT THEM TO COME AFTER *YOU* INSTEAD OF THOSE INNOCENT PEOPLE, YOU'VE GOT TO PUT THIS ON.

I NEED TO GET THESE PEOPLE TO SAFETY! CAN YOU KEEP THE ROCK MONSTERS OCCUPIED UNTIL THEN?

THAT'S RIGHT. I CAN ROCK THIS LOOK, TOO.

TRAS

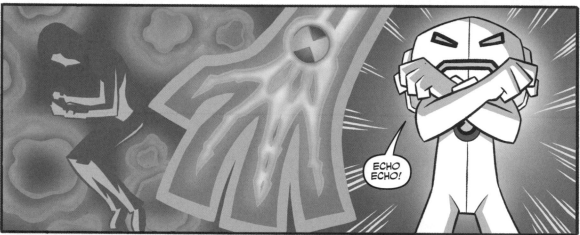

IT'S TIME TO GO ULTIMATE!

ULTIMATE ECHO ECHO!

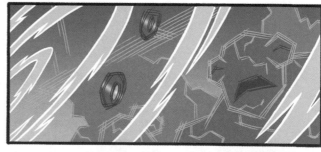

ULTIMATE HUMUNGOUSAUR

Ultimate Humungousaur is bigger and stronger than ever before! He also has spikes on his body.

ALIEN FACTS

- Formed when Humungousaur hits his Omnitrix symbol.

- Has blue armour and a slightly hunched back.

- Can fire missiles from his hands.

HERO

HUMUNGOUSAUR

Humungousaur's thick dinosaur-skin protects him from most attacks.

HUMUNGO-SEARCH

Ultimate Humungousaur is looking for some good and bad guys. Look for all the names in this grid. They can read up, down, across, backwards and diagonally.

F	O	R	E	V	E	R	K	N	I	G	H	T	S
R	U	S	T	B	R	T	A	E	T	H	E	T	I
W	T	F	M	X	T	L	U	L	M	A	N	J	S
I	J	D	C	T	K	L	M	O	S	G	N	J	E
L	B	J	U	L	I	E	Z	D	S	G	F	A	M
L	T	A	L	C	N	O	K	T	S	R	G	H	E
H	F	U	T	N	B	J	G	O	E	E	M	G	N
A	L	T	V	M	D	E	W	T	R	G	A	A	N
R	O	J	O	C	K	P	E	U	P	O	X	J	I
A	S	Z	T	K	M	N	N	X	E	R	U	K	A
N	A	C	K	E	V	I	N	B	N	D	F	H	T
G	C	H	A	R	M	C	A	S	T	E	R	E	P
U	T	C	A	T	D	V	A	E	D	M	A	L	A
E	C	S	E	V	E	N	S	E	V	E	N	T	C

FOREVER KNIGHTS

SEVEN SEVEN

WILL HARANGUE

MAX

AGGREGOR

ROJO

KEVIN

GWEN

ZOMBOZO

SSSERPENT

CAPTAIN NEMESIS

JULIE

CHARMCASTER

CHECK YOUR ANSWERS ON PAGE 255.

TERRASPIN

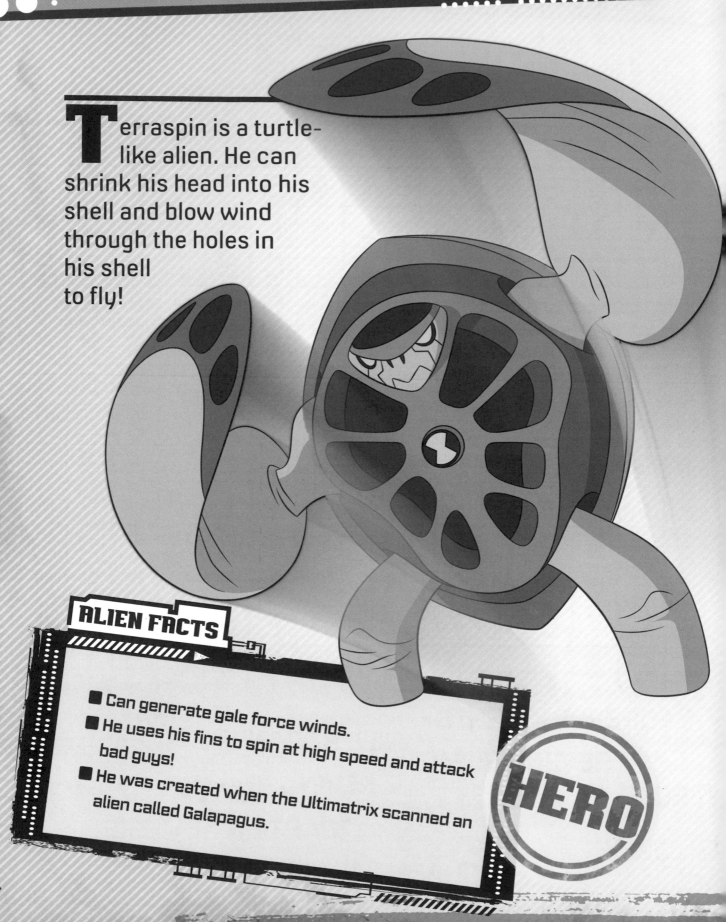

Terraspin is a turtle-like alien. He can shrink his head into his shell and blow wind through the holes in his shell to fly!

ALIEN FACTS

■ Can generate gale force winds.
■ He uses his fins to spin at high speed and attack bad guys!
■ He was created when the Ultimatrix scanned an alien called Galapagus.

HERO

TERRASPIN'S SEARCH

Terraspin's feeling a bit dizzy. Can you help him complete this puzzle? See if you can fit the words in the grid below. One has been done for you.

5 LETTERS:
WINDY

6 LETTERS:
BREEZY
CLOUDY

7 LETTERS:
TORNADO
TYPHOON
CYCLONE

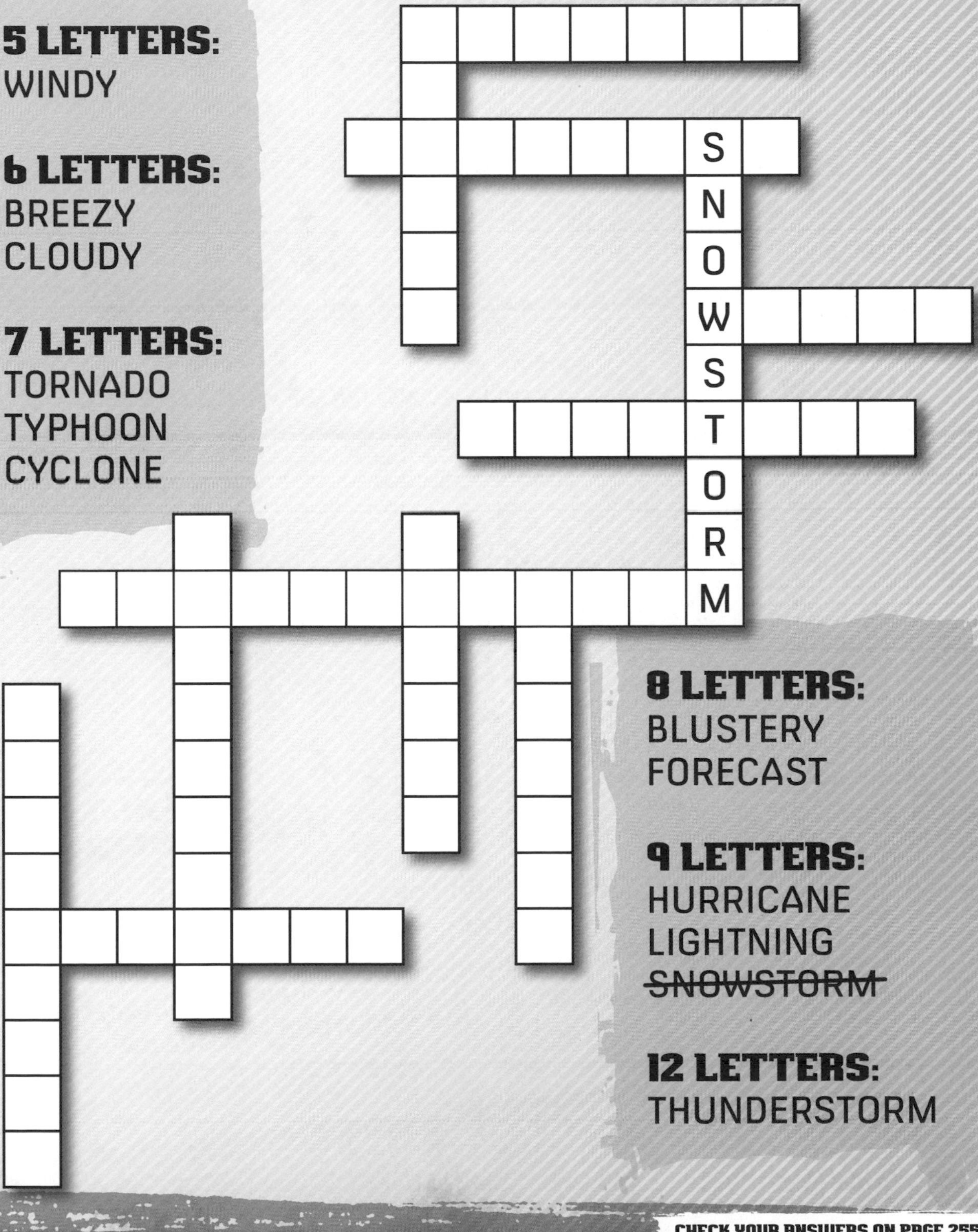

8 LETTERS:
BLUSTERY
FORECAST

9 LETTERS:
HURRICANE
LIGHTNING
~~SNOWSTORM~~

12 LETTERS:
THUNDERSTORM

CHECK YOUR ANSWERS ON PAGE 255.

WATER HAZARD

Water Hazard looks a bit like a crab. He's able to breathe underwater and can shoot highly-pressurized water blasts from his palms.

HERO

ALIEN FACTS

- Can control water and mould it into all sorts of shapes.
- His armour-like body is extremely tough.
- He was created when the Ultimatrix scanned an alien called Bivalvan.

WATER CANNON

Which of Water Hazard's water blasts will knock Aggregor out? The most powerful route is the one with the largest total when the numbers are added together. Write the totals for each route in the spaces at the bottom.

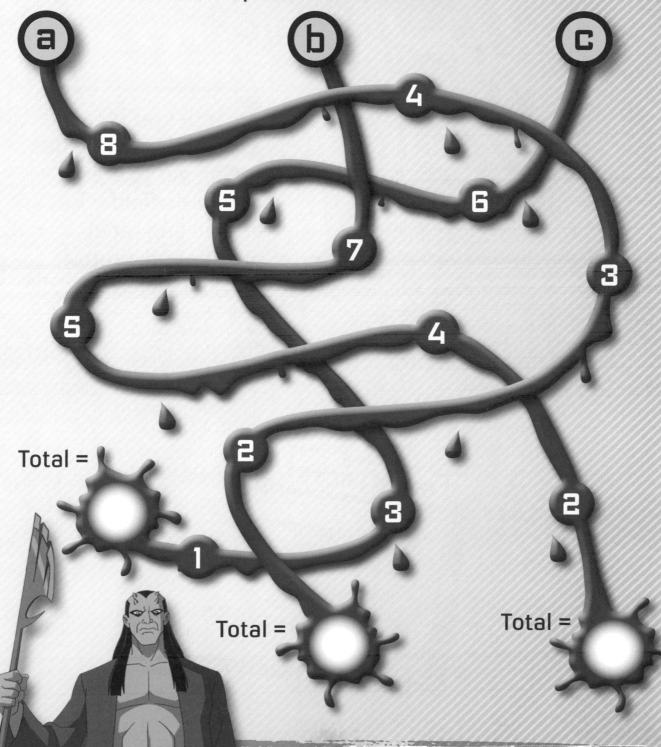

Total =

Total =

Total =

LODESTAR

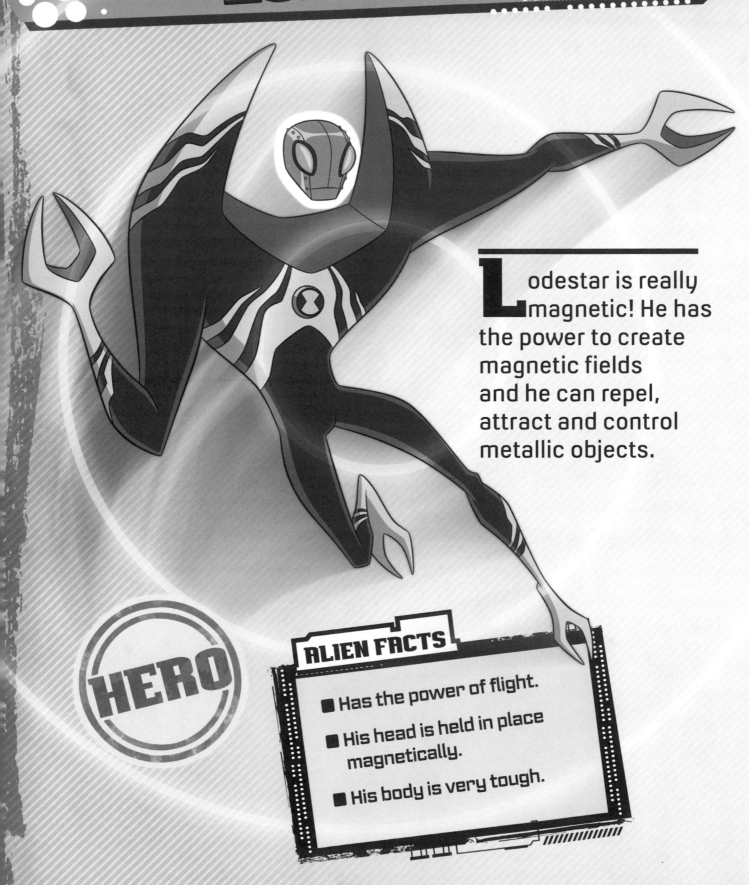

Lodestar is really magnetic! He has the power to create magnetic fields and he can repel, attract and control metallic objects.

HERO

ALIEN FACTS

- Has the power of flight.
- His head is held in place magnetically.
- His body is very tough.

MAGNETIC ART

Find a sticker of Lodestar and place it on the page.
Then use the sticker as a guide and fill your Lodestar
picture with awesome colours!

VILLAINS

Ever since the world found out about Ben's powers, a lot of his old enemies have been crawling out of the woodwork. Here are just a few of them. But there's also one major new threat out there ...

AGGREGOR

is the main villain in Ultimate Alien. He is mysterious and has absorbing powers. He kidnapped five aliens (Bivalvan, Andreas, P'andor, Ra'ad and Galapagus) from the Andromeda Galaxy, but they escaped from his ship to Earth. Now Aggregor is hunting them down one by one. He wants to drain the aliens' powers and claim what he calls 'the ultimate prize'.

VILLAIN

FOREVER KNIGHTS

Ben first met the Forever Knights in Alien Force. They are a secret society formed during the Middle Ages and they seek alien technology for their own use. They wear a full suit of metal body armour.

VILLAIN

VILLAIN

WILL HARANGUE

Will Harangue is a wealthy and power-crazy TV presenter. He's jealous of Ben's fame and sees him as a menace, not a superhero.

CAPTAIN NEMESIS

Captain Nemesis used to be a superhero and Ben was one of his biggest fans. But Nemesis' fame has corrupted him, and now he's all bad. He is very strong, able to fly with a jet pack and he can boost up his suit with devastating results.

VILLAIN

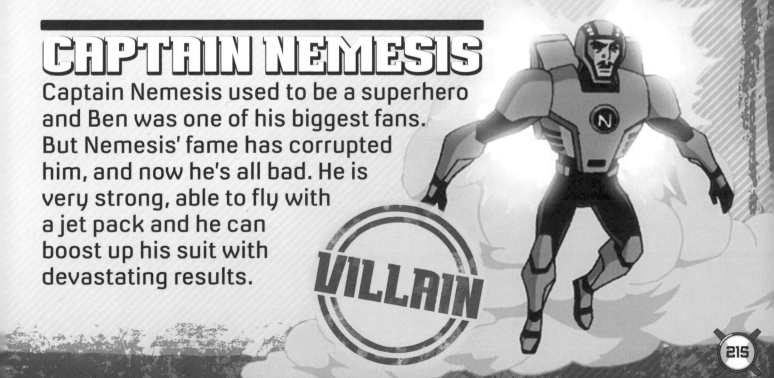

ZOMBOZO

Ben first met Zombozo six years ago and he's back to cause more trouble. He's a scary clown with plenty of tricks up his sleeve, including a trick buzzer that stuns his victims. Zombozo often teams up with Charmcaster and Vulkanus.

CHARMCASTER

Charmcaster is a witch who Ben and Gwen came up against when they were younger. Now she's back and has a team of lumbering rock monsters under her control. Charmcaster can also scatter strange seeds which quickly sprout into huge vines.

VULKANUS

The gang first met Vulkanus long ago. He's an alien technology dealer who has lots of blaster weapons. He looks huge in his robotic, hi-tech suit – but really he's just a tiny orange alien beneath all that bulky armour!

WHAT NEXT?

Ben's come face-to-face with Ssserpent, a creepy half-man, half-cobra creature. Use this space to draw what you think happens next. Be sure to choose a powerful alien transformation for Ben!

RATH

Rath is like a boxer and is Ben's angriest alien! He is also very powerful and has a razor-sharp claw on each hand.

ALIEN FACTS

- Looks like a tiger – but he has no tail.

- His claws are sharp enough to cut rock.

- He alters Ben's personality the most among the aliens.

HERO

RATH'S SPEECH

Rath's being snarly! He's saying something, but it's all in code. Use the code breaker to work out what he's saying.

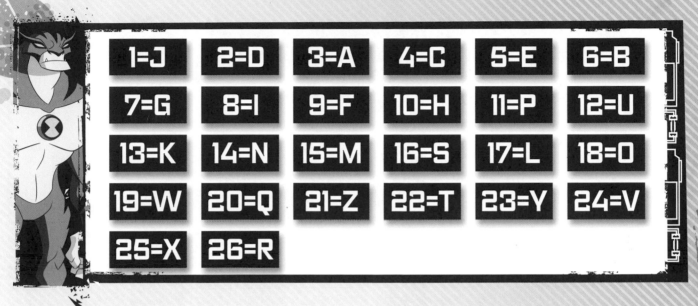

1=J	2=D	3=A	4=C	5=E	6=B
7=G	8=I	9=F	10=H	11=P	12=U
13=K	14=N	15=M	16=S	17=L	18=O
19=W	20=Q	21=Z	22=T	23=Y	24=V
25=X	26=R				

The code

17 / 5 / 22   15 / 5   22 / 5 / 17 / 17   23 / 18 / 12

16 / 18 / 15 / 5 / 22 / 10 / 8 / 14 / 7 !

_ _ _   _ _   _ _ _ _   _ _ _

_ _ _ _ _ _ _ _ _ !

HAHAHAHA! HAHAHAHA!

WHAT'S SO FUNNY?

YOU!

APPARENTLY THERE WAS A GARDENER HIDING IN ONE OF THE SHACKS. CAUGHT THE WHOLE THING ON HIS CELLPHONE.

BUT... UH... HOW? I WAS THE ONLY ONE THERE.

AW, MAN.

BUT ON THE BRIGHT SIDE, YOU'RE THE NUMBER-ONE DOWNLOAD ON THE INTERNET.

GREAT.

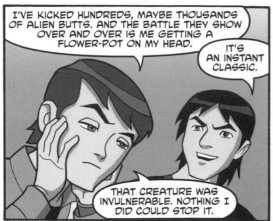

I'VE KICKED HUNDREDS, MAYBE THOUSANDS OF ALIEN BUTTS. AND THE BATTLE THEY SHOW OVER AND OVER IS ME GETTING A FLOWER-POT ON MY HEAD.

IT'S AN INSTANT CLASSIC.

THAT CREATURE WAS INVULNERABLE. NOTHING I DID COULD STOP IT.

COME ON, LET'S GET SOME ICE CREAM.

NAH.

DOUBLE SCOOPS?

OKAY.

SUMMER ICE CREAM

HA HA HA HA!!

HEY, IT'S THE FLOWER-POT DUDE!

I SAVE THE WORLD A MILLION TIMES, AND NOW I'M "FLOWER-POT DUDE"?

BUH-BYE!

YOU GOT THAT ON VIDEO, RIGHT?

WHAT, NO CAMERAS? NO CELL-PHONE? NOBODY? AW, C'MON.

END

SIZZLE

COMIC CREATOR

Make your own action-packed Ben 10 comic by creating pictures with your stickers and drawings in the panels below. Add speech bubbles to make your story really come to life!

You will need:
• Character stickers – both good guys and baddies
• Coloured pencils or pens to draw in the scenes
• An idea for an ace story!

Title:

....

Written and illustrated by:

....

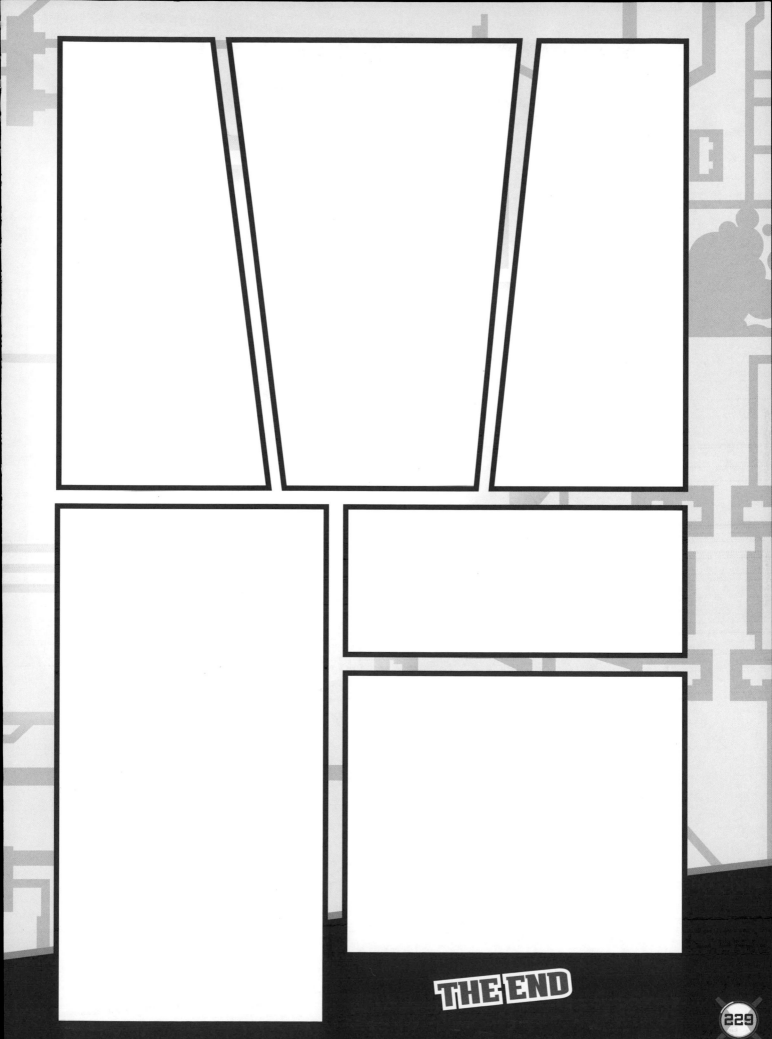

THE END

AMPFIBIAN

Ampfibian's powers are electric, but he's also a very fast swimmer who can breathe underwater. Jellyfish-like Ampfibian uses his long tendrils to zap victims.

ALIEN FACTS

- He can drain electricity from objects.

- He's able to travel as electric current through power lines.

- He was created when the Ultimatrix scanned an alien called Ra'ad.

HERO

AMPED ART

Draw over the lines to finish this picture of Ampfibian.
Add some awesome waves in the background, too!

NRG

NRG is a radioactive energy life-form contained in the toughest armour. He has heat-based powers that allow him to melt through solid metal and rock.

ALIEN FACTS

- Can shoot energy beams through the holes in his helmet.
- When he's released from his armour, he can create intense heat.
- He was formed when the Ultimatrix scanned an alien called P'andor.

HERO

TOP ALIEN

All of Ben's aliens are totally cool – but which is your favourite? Draw it here, and add some stickers if you want.

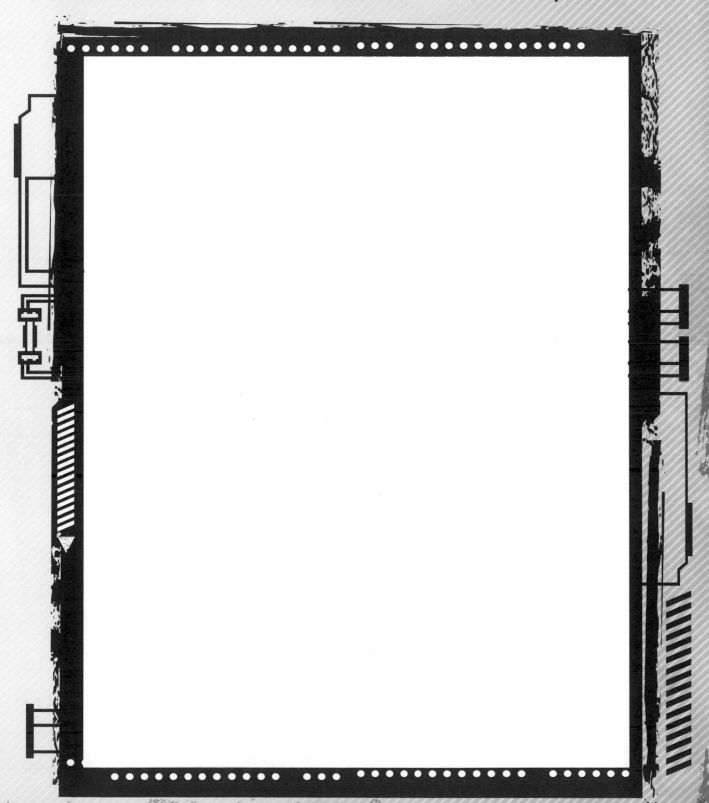

MAZE CRAZE

Vulkanus has created a weapon to destroy the solar system. Can you show Kevin the quickest way through the maze to his secret hideout? Avoid the Forever Knights along the way!

CHECK YOUR ANSWER ON PAGE 255.

ULTIMATE
ECHO ECHO

ULTIMATE UPGRADES:

- Shoots amplifiers to create powerful sonic blasts
- Projects sound waves to fly at the speed of sound

HERO

ULTIMATE SWAMPFIRE

HERO

ULTIMATE UPGRADES:

- More intense, blue-coloured fire
- Generates firebombs, nova blasts and fiery tornadoes

ULTIMATE BIG CHILL

HERO

ULTIMATE UPGRADES:

- Shoots ice flames, which burn then freeze enemies
- Quicker freezing abilities
- Faster phasing through objects and flying

ULTIMATE SPIDERMONKEY

ULTIMATE UPGRADES:

- Super strength
- Shoots more webbing from his mouth
- Sticks to walls

HERO

ULTIMATE HUMUNGOUSAUR

ULTIMATE UPGRADES:

- Twice as strong
- Instantly grows to 37 metres tall
- Fires explosives from hands
- Spiked mace on tail

HERO

ULTIMATE CANNONBOLT

ULTIMATE UPGRADES:

- Forms sharp spikes when in ball form
- Ultra-strong armour even withstands radiation
- Bigger and faster

HERO

ARMODRILLO

Armodrillo is a bulky robotic alien with drills in his arms. The tremors he creates can cause earthquakes, and he can move easily through solid rock.

ALIEN FACTS

- Can drill into the earth using his very strong arms.

- His main form of attack is a powerful 'pneumatic drill' punch.

- He was created when the Ultimatrix scanned an alien called Andreas.

ARMODRILLO ART

Find a sticker of Armodrillo, then use it as a guide to colour him in!

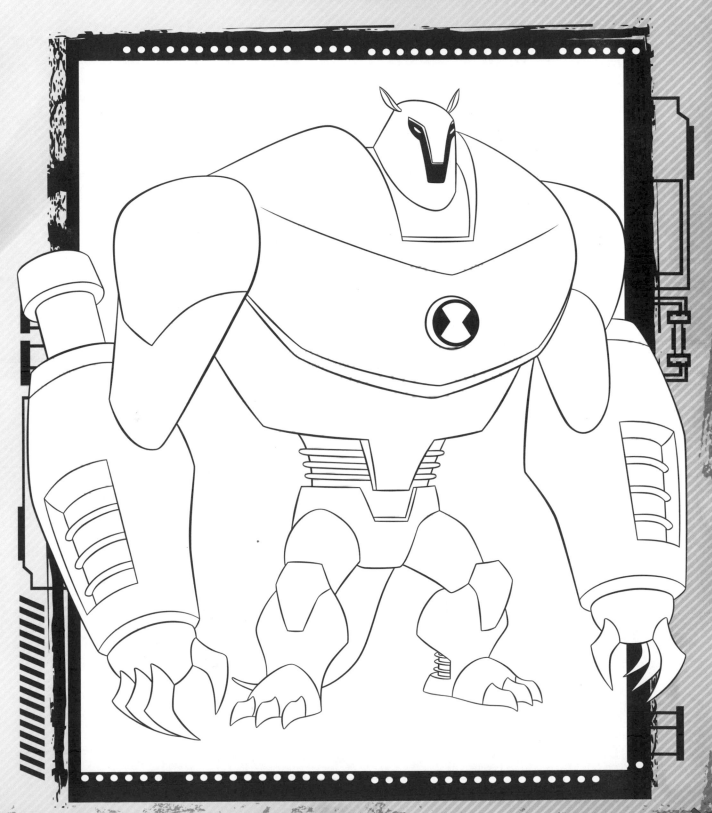

NANOMECH

Nanomech is a tiny carbon-based life form. He is small enough to enter machines! But he packs a powerful punch by firing out powerful energy bolts.

ALIEN FACTS

- Can become tiny and shrink to sub-atomic particle size.

- This little guy is able to fly.

- He comes from a hive of insects, but is human in shape.

HERO

NANOMECH COLOUR

Carefully copy over the lines to bring Nanomech to life!

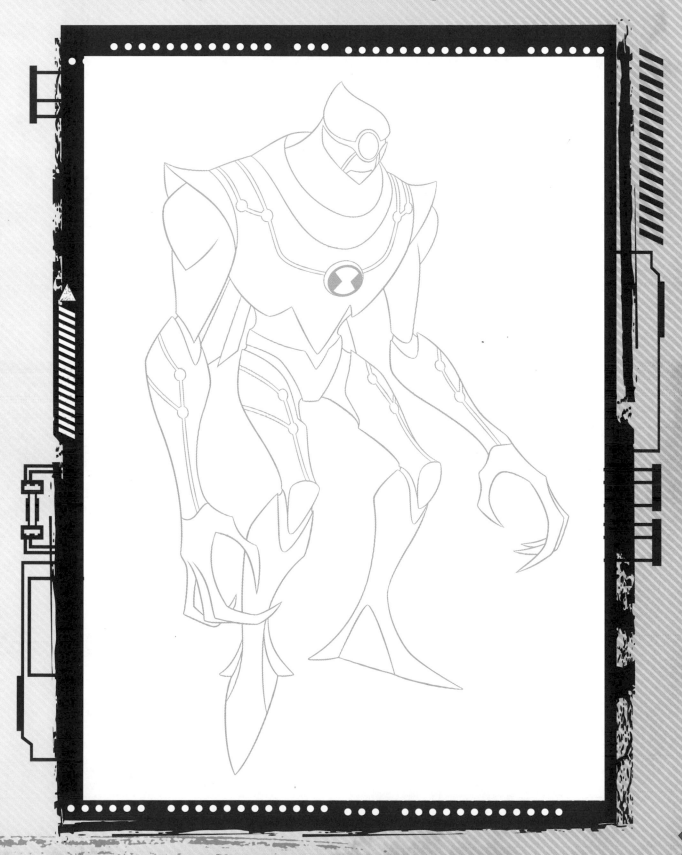

HERO TIME

Do you know Cannonbolt from ChromaStone? What's Kevin's last name? See how well you've been paying attention by having a crack at Ben's ultimate quiz!

1 Which Ultimate Alien can shoot fire bombs?
a. Spidermonkey
b. Echo Echo
c. Swampfire

2 What is the name of the evil creature that is half-man, half-cobra?
a. Shoe Horn
b. Ssserpent
c. Snake Charm

3 What is Kevin's new form of transportation?
a. Jet
b. Hoverboard
c. Motorcycle

4 Name all the alien forms that have Ultimate versions.

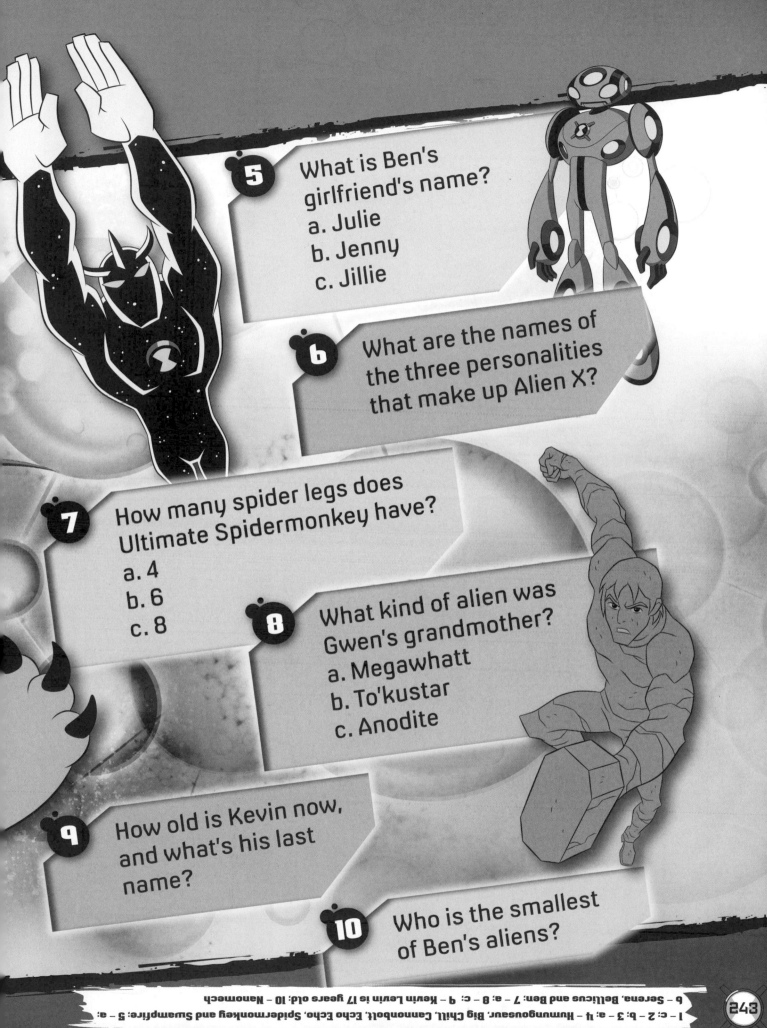

5 What is Ben's girlfriend's name?
a. Julie
b. Jenny
c. Jillie

6 What are the names of the three personalities that make up Alien X?

7 How many spider legs does Ultimate Spidermonkey have?
a. 4
b. 6
c. 8

8 What kind of alien was Gwen's grandmother?
a. Megawhatt
b. To'kustar
c. Anodite

9 How old is Kevin now, and what's his last name?

10 Who is the smallest of Ben's aliens?

1 – c; 2 – b; 3 – a; 4 – Humungousaur, Big Chill, Cannonbolt, Echo Echo, Spidermonkey and Swampfire; 5 – a; 6 – Serena, Bellicus and Ben; 7 – a; 8 – c; 9 – Kevin Levin is 17 years old; 10 – Nanomech

243

AW, MAN. WHAT NOW?

BREAKING NEWS

written by JAKE BLACK
art by ETHEN BEAVERS
color by HEROIC AGE
lettering by TRAVIS LANHAM
edited by SEAN RYAN
BEN 10 ULTIMATE ALIEN
created by MAN OF ACTION

YOU THINK I'D BE USED TO ALIEN INVASIONS BY NOW!

WE HAVE ARRIVED ON EARTH, HOME OF THE GREAT BEN TENNYSON.

I'M BEN TENNYSON.

AND I'M GORPHAX, WITH THE GALACTIC NEWS AGENCY. WE'VE COME TO DO A STORY ON YOU!

COOL!

THIS IS WHERE I GO TO SCHOOL...WHEN I'M NOT FIGHTING BIG, BAD ALIEN MONSTERS.

FASCINATING!

HERE THE HEROIC TEEN TRAINS HIS MIND THROUGH INTENSE BATTLE SIMULATIONS.

AW, MAN! I'M GOING TO LOSE TO THESE FREAKS!

IT IS AMAZING HOW TENNYSON KEEPS HIS ENERGY UP!

SERIOUSLY. FOLLOWING ME AROUND WHILE I DO BORING STUFF LIKE GO TO SCHOOL AND EAT IS GETTING A LITTLE OLD.

THIS YOUR RIDE HOME?

I'VE NEVER SEEN IT BEFORE IN MY LIFE.

THEN I THINK WE'VE GOT A PROBLEM!

DNALIENS! THEY'RE REALLY DANGEROUS! WE'VE GOT TO GET YOU OUT OF HERE!

IT'S ULTIMATE HERO TIME!

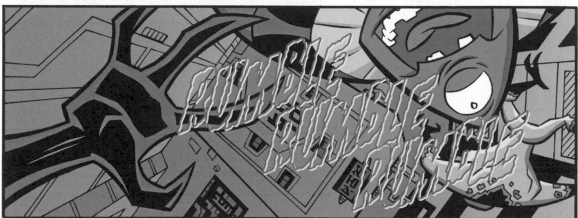

SEVERAL WEEKS LATER.

WHAT ARE YOU DOING, BEN?

THAT GALACTIC NEWS STORY ABOUT ME IS BEING UPLOADED TONIGHT.

BEN TENNYSON. HE'S KNOWN THROUGHOUT THE GALAXY AS ONE OF THE GREATEST HEROES OF ALL TIME.

BUT WHO'S THE REAL BEN TENNYSON?

"WE INVESTIGATED THE STORY AND DISCOVERED HE'S NOT WHAT YOU THINK."

"WHEN AN ARMY OF DNALIENS ATTACKED, HE RAN AWAY IN FEAR."

"IT WAS UP TO ME TO SAVE THE DAY.

"SO I, A LOWLY, HUMBLE REPORTER, ACTED IN THE ONLY WAY I KNEW HOW.

"I SAVED THE SO-CALLED HERO. AND PERHAPS THE ENTIRE GALAXY."

WOW, BEN, THAT'S...

THEY SHOWED THE REAL BEN 10! IF IT'S ON THE NEWS, IT MUST BE TRUE!

I NEED A PRESS AGENT.

THE END

ALIEN ROUND-UP!

It's time to say goodbye to Ben and all the awesome aliens you've met along the way. Take a look at this alien chart and see if you can remember all of their names. Search back through the book for help and write in the names as you remember them.

---------- ---------- ---------- ----------

---------- ---------- ---------- ----------

---------- ---------- ---------- ----------

Until next time, comrade — I couldn't have beaten the bad guys without you. You've been **AWESOME!**

ANSWERS

Page 29: ALIEN MAZE

Page 36-37: TO THE RESCUE

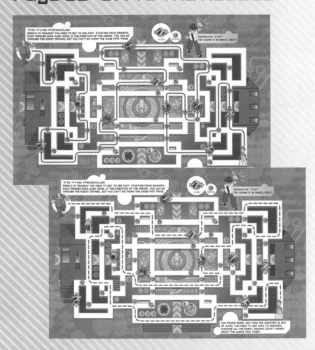

Page 58: WHERE'S BEN?

Ben's name is repeated 12 times

Page 67 FIT 'EM IN

The extra word is 'dweeb'

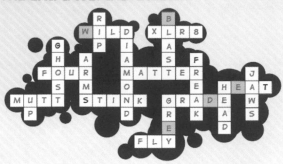

Page 107 ECHO DUPLICATION

Echo Echo's name is repeated 7 times

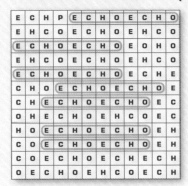

Page 121: ZONE IN

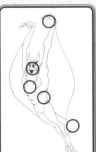

Page 136: COSMIC SEARCH

PAGE 142: RESCUE MISSION

Page 190–191: THE FINAL BATTLE

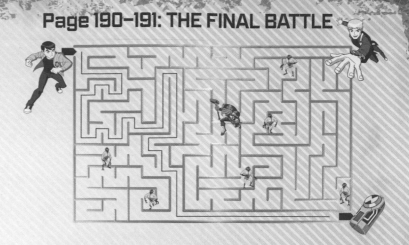

PAGE 163: CHROMA-SEARCH

ChromaStone uses lasers

S	A	B	I	G	C	H	I	L	L	R	S
A	W	M	T	E	N	R	O	P	T	B	T
L	P	A	E	C	H	V	G	O	O	P	E
I	L	X	M	N	S	B	N	U	B	E	M
N	M	W	N	P	R	H	E	O	S	L	O
M	C	A	B	B	F	A	N	L	R	R	L
B	H	S	L	L	R	I	S	A	P	E	P
X	R	T	O	I	A	L	R	J	I	U	J
B	O	A	P	L	E	X	R	E	G	S	B
L	M	A	I	S	E	N	R	T	W	S	E
F	A	L	E	N	E	S	X	R	E	W	N
G	S	D	R	V	S	L	I	A	N	Q	I
W	T	F	R	B	R	T	N	Y	R	R	E
D	O	S	F	N	J	B	O	S	T	N	N
T	N	E	K	E	V	I	N	R	N	E	X
M	E	R	S	A	N	P	O	V	M	P	P

Page 207: HUMUNGO-SEARCH

F	O	R	E	V	E	R	K	N	I	G	H	T	S
R	U	S	T	B	R	T	A	E	T	H	E	T	
W	T	F	M	X	T	L	U	L	M	A	N	J	S
I	J	D	C	T	K	L	M	O	S	G	N	J	E
L	B	J	U	L	I	E	Z	D	S	G	F	A	M
L	T	A	L	C	N	O	K	T	S	R	G	H	E
H	F	U	T	N	B	J	G	O	E	E	M	G	N
A	L	T	V	M	D	E	W	T	R	G	A	A	N
R	O	J	O	C	K	P	E	U	P	O	X	J	I
A	S	Z	T	K	M	N	N	X	E	R	U	K	A
N	A	C	K	E	V	I	N	B	N	D	F	H	T
G	C	H	A	R	M	C	A	S	T	E	R	E	P
U	T	C	A	T	D	V	A	E	D	M	A	L	A
E	C	S	E	V	E	N	S	E	V	E	N	T	C

PAGE 185: CYBER GRID

Page 209: TERRASPIN'S SEARCH

Page 234: MAZE CRAZE